C000076366

JESUS AND THE CHRIST

Stephen R. White

Jesus and the Christ
Unity, Necessity and Contingency

the columba press

First published in 2012 by
the columba press
55A Spruce Avenue, Stillorgan Industrial Park,
Blackrock, Co Dublin

Cover by Bill Bolger
Origination by The Columba Press
Printed in Ireland by
Dublin
ISBN 978 1 85607 742 2

Copyright © 2012, Stephen R. White

Contents

PART ONE

The Possibility of Becoming

Introduction

Biblical scholars and commentators have frequently noted the almost spiral nature of the patterning in St John's gospel, the way in which the writer takes up and explores an idea, and then apparently leaves it behind only to revisit it later with a different slant or on a different plane. Stephen Verney explores this patterning particularly deftly in his moving meditation on this gospel, *Water into Wine*.[1] And this same image of the spiral is an illuminating one not solely for St John's gospel, but for the whole understanding of the task of theology.

In one sense this must inevitably be so, for there is only a finite (although very substantial) number of avenues and topics which theology can reasonably pursue. We cannot forever be inventing endless new branches of the subject, but must return time and again to the 'given' data: that is, scripture, revelation, personal experience of God in prayer and in daily living, and the historic doctrinal content and tradition of our faith. In another sense, however, this is no limitation at all, for we do not revisit familiar territory merely because there is nowhere else to go, but rather because that territory, however well-known, holds, for each new generation, almost endless possibilities for new vistas and with them new visions and insights into seemingly infinite reservoirs of meaning.

The person of Jesus of Nazareth constitutes one such theme which has been revisited time and again in every generation for the past two thousand years. Indeed, even at the very beginning, one gospel was not enough to begin to explore the possibilities opened up by the striking and enigmatic figure of Jesus: the Bible holds no fewer than four gospels, and there is also a substantial number of extra-canonical gospels (admittedly of varying reliability!). Similarly, the New Testament epistles likewise seek to explore what it means to live life in the light of Jesus' birth, ministry, death and resurrection, and they too, therefore, contain christologies in varying degrees of depth and completeness.[2] This continual refocusing on the person and work of Jesus has been conducted in several ways and in order to seek to answer a wide range of questions.

At what is perhaps the most basic level – that of historicity – there have been periodic efforts to ascertain the historical reliability of the gospel records, or to extrapolate from them an acceptably accurate picture of the words and actions of the 'Jesus of history'. Most famous among these efforts has been Albert Schweitzer's (and others') so-called 'Quest for the Historical Jesus', which has itself been paralleled in more recent years by a 'New Quest'. Allied to this have been attempts to interpret and account for Jesus' self-understanding and sense of divine vocation, or to evaluate the relationship between the 'Jesus of history' and the 'Christ of faith'.

On a more overtly theological and / or metaphysical level, there have been repeated discussions (often heated and partisan) on the status of certain doctrinal elements (resting on a historical foundation) surrounding the figure of Jesus, such as parthenogenesis, resurrection and ascension, to say nothing of efforts to unravel the mysteries of pre-existence and the ultimate 'How?' of the incarnation.

One might think, therefore, that the subject of Jesus had become by now theologically – though not, of course, devotionally – exhausted, in the manner of a mine whose vein of precious mineral has finally been 'worked out'. And yet the amazing and perennially wonderful thing is that this never seems to be the case. Always this compelling, challenging and life-changing figure of Jesus tempts us back again and again to interrogate him once more with the questions, pre-suppositions and ideologies of a new generation, and always ever-new and ever-exciting answers (or at least, in keeping with the Jesus of scripture, further questions!) seem to be returned.

Christology – as also is theology in general – is an area wherein one is advised to tread carefully, for the whole subject-matter of theology is, as I have argued in an earlier book, ultimately and necessarily beyond us, a fact to which we will return in the conclusion to this study.[3] This facet of the theological task is deftly captured in a recent book by Stanley Hauerwas. With

characteristic lightness of touch he notes with gentle irony that:
'... theology is a discipline whose subject should always put in
doubt the very idea that those who practise it know what they
are doing.'[4] And with regard to christology in particular,
Hauerwas is equally explicit. Referring to an early stage in his
career he comments:

> At the time, I certainly did not have a well-worked-out
> christology. Indeed, I still do not. I am not even sure I believe
> in anyone having a well-worked-out christology.[5]

In the face, then, of the wealth of thinking, both theological and
devotional, which has exercised some of the greatest minds
across the ages, and bearing in mind the dangers of the task as
detailed by Hauerwas, it may be surprising that anyone – and
least of all one who is not a full-time professional academic theologian – should have the temerity to venture once more into the
domain of christology; and yet there is, it seems to me, one crucial
area in particular to which insufficient attention has been paid,
and which, depending upon one's viewpoint, has profound
consequences not only for christology itself, but also for a number of other areas both of theology and Christian praxis. This
area, as the title of this book suggests, is the precise nature of the
relationship between the man, Jesus of Nazareth (or Jesus-bar-
Joseph), and the divine figure of the 'Christ', with all its connotations of pre-existence and eternal identity with God.

   In one sense, of course, this relationship has been at the heart
of the vast bulk of christological thinking and writing from the
earliest times, being, as it must be, central to debates such as
'one nature or two natures' and the human/divine dichotomy
epitomised in the Arian and Apollinarian (to say nothing of the
more extreme Docetist) controversies. For all this, however,
there is one specific question which has, for the most part been
neglected, largely, I suspect, because the answer has been assumed to be an *a priori* given of faith.

   The question is simply this: are Jesus and the Christ necessarily one and the same, or is the union between them (a union so
profound that we may properly speak, as the Christian tradition
has always done, of Jesus Christ) something entirely contingent
and which, might, therefore, had things turned out differently,

not have been the case? It is a question which has been at least
hinted at in some recent christological studies. Thus in a major
work from the mid 1990s, Gerald O'Collins has this to say:

> Even if we know with certainty many historical truths, they
> always remain contingent or accidental. These historical
> events, the truth of which we have learned and established,
> neither had to be at all nor had to be precisely the way they
> were. In principle things could have gone differently in the
> life and career of Alexander the Great, Augustine, Jesus and
> Julius Caesar. As such, historical truths neither enjoy the status
> of necessary, universal truths of reason, nor can they work to
> prove such truths of reason. But is that so tragic? ... is it a fatal
> admission to grant that our knowledge of Jesus' career does
> not rise 'above' the level of contingent truths? Strictly speak-
> ing, he could have done, said, and suffered different things.[6]

Here, as in a variety of other places in similar studies, this vital
question is broached, but is then largely ignored, and yet it is my
contention that it is, at the present time, precisely this question
which needs to be explored most fully because of the possibility
which it offers of leading us to a much needed new and more
fruitful way of approaching christology.

Some sort of new approach is felt indeed to be overdue even
within the world of academic theology itself. Karl-Josef Kuschel
expresses it particularly appositely towards the conclusion of
his magisterial study, *Born Before All Time?* He writes:

> The church's christology now seems exposed to a crisis of
> plausibility and acceptance of unknown dimensions – while
> at the same time the figure of Jesus himself is affirmed to an
> astonishing degree ... It is ... connected with a theological
> language which is often alien to the world, with an over-
> complex way of thinking, with forced solutions to problems
> which many people no longer raise as they are raised there.
> In short, it has to do with a theology which has become sterile,
> which often only solves problems that it has made for itself,
> and has ready answers to questions which hardly anyone
> asks any more.[7]

This book is intended to represent precisely such a necessary new approach to the person and work of Jesus Christ, and one which attempts to explore most especially his person in thought categories which are meaningful to the contemporary mind. It is intended, in short, to explore the question of unity, contingency and necessity, and with it the ramifications of some of the possible answers to it. The thinking contained here may perhaps stimulate some or annoy others, and some may even find themselves longing for the good old days when heretics were burned at the stake. I would, however, argue strongly for the ultimate orthodoxy of the unfamiliar and potentially threatening or disturbing views advanced here, and, in the end, perhaps, some may even find that the Christ is to be met with more fully and more life-enhancingly in contingency than in necessity, and faith may, by unfamiliar paths, be enriched rather than diminished. Such at least is the purpose of this work, and the hope in which it is written.

Notes
1. Stephen Verney, *Water into Wine*, London, Fount Paperbacks, 1985.
2. See, for example, Frank J. Matera, *New Testament Christology*, Louisville & London, Westminster John Knox Press, 1999.
3. See, Stephen R. White, *A Space for Unknowing: The Place of Agnosis in Faith*, Dublin, The Columba Press, 2006.
4. Stanley Hauerwas, *Hannah's Child: A Theologian's Memoir*, London, SCM Press, 2010, p ix.
5. Ibid., p 59.
6. Gerald O'Collins, SJ, *Christology: A Biblical, Historical and Systematic Study of Jesus*, Oxford, Oxford University Press, 1995, p 9.
7. Karl-Josef Kuschel, *Born Before All Time? The Dispute over Christ's Origin*, London, SCM Press, 1992, pp. 485-6.

CHAPTER ONE

Framing the Question

At the close of the introduction I posed, in outline, the basic question which forms the reason behind this study, namely, the question of the necessity or the contingency of the union between human and divine in the person of Jesus Christ. Before proceeding any further, however, it is important to refine this question somewhat, and to distinguish it from one or two related (but ultimately different) questions with which it might otherwise easily become confused.

Perhaps the two most essential issues in distinction from which the question needs to be classified are those of the ontological status of Jesus' Sonship and Messiahship, and the related age-old 'degree' or 'kind' christological debate. The issue of whether Jesus differs from us in 'degree' or in 'kind' is one of the oldest christological controversies of all, being, in effect, foundational for many of the disputes over christology during the patristic period. Indeed, it has become so ingrained as a core christological question that it was actually the subject of the very first doctrine essay which I was required to write during my days at theological college!

Essentially, the answer which one returns to this question depends upon the relative values which one places respectively on the humanity and divinity of Jesus. A heavy stress on his humanity will tend naturally to produce a degree christology, whilst an approach 'from above' stressing his divinity will generate a christology founded upon a difference in kind. Traditionally, orthodox Christianity has come to a kind of uneasy balance between the two positions, rejecting on the one hand the over-humanising tendency of Arianism or any of its theological offspring, and eschewing equally on the other hand the divinising of humanity to the extent that it becomes a form of Docetism. Thus the classical stance of orthodoxy (as expressed, for example, in painstaking detail in the so-called Athanasian Creed) is that Jesus Christ is 'fully' human and 'fully' divine, thereby setting in motion the mystery of incarnational metaphysics which theologians have spent much of the past two thousand years trying to elucidate in satisfactory and more or less intelligible terms.

There is, though, it seems to me, still one central flaw which undercuts and vitiates the whole discussion between degree and kind christologies, and this is simply that the entire conversation begins from what is, ontologically speaking, a very dubious premise, and from what is in my view quite certainly the wrong place. Thus the underlying premise is that the nature of Jesus – and of every other individual – is eternally (and therefore unchangeably) of one ontological 'species' or another, and that consequently differences of degree and kind are the only conceivable forms of difference between Jesus and ourselves which can possibly exist. It is as if every being must exist in a static and unalterable ontological pigeon-hole which thereby itself defines the terms of any potential debate about humanity and divinity. Metaphysically speaking, this may well be very attractive since it posits very neat lines of demarcation between the two realms of the human and the divine – whichever side of the divide one happens to inhabit – and provides for a tidily circumscribed intellectual context within which questions may be framed and debates conducted.

What it ignores, however, whether by design or as a result of simple oversight, is an entirely alien 'other' and potentially disruptive set of possibilities based on precisely the opposite opening premise: namely, that the 'nature' of Jesus, and therefore even of the whole of humanity, is (or perhaps more properly, in the case of Jesus as being in the past, was,) not ontologically fixed, and that there are many other grounds of difference between him and ourselves than merely those of degree and kind.

It is not appropriate, as yet, to investigate the nature of these potential differences too fully – more grounds for such difference will become apparent as this study proceeds – but their possibility should at least be noted. If such a conception of difference is to be allowed at all, then clearly the question needs to be asked: in what might such difference consist if it is not to be couched in the traditional categories of degree and kind? One answer to this question – and it is my own preferred one – begins from the concept of 'potential' and the process of 'becoming'.

It is perhaps putting the theological cart before the horse, but it is worth pointing out that in contexts other than the incarnation itself this is already a well-founded and much respected pattern of thinking, especially as far as our devotional life is concerned, and thus we should not be afraid of it or too quick to reject it *per se*. The concept itself is not new, only I think, its particular application to incarnation and Christhood – and if it resonates with our own spiritual odyssey, then why not with that of Jesus himself? Unless, of course, we stick doggedly to the notion that he is different from us in kind.

What, then, of becoming and potential on the wider theological stage and in our own experience? In large measure the great nineteenth century theological thinker F. D. Maurice encapsulated the profoundly true and yet paradoxical nature of these interrelated concepts in his celebrated statement, 'Become what you are'. In one sense we are God's children, redeemed, sanctified and caught up into the life of the divine: in another sense – as from St Paul onwards we have all known within ourselves all too clearly – we have a long way to go to make this potential a reality. Another excellent parallel would be the 'already existing' and yet 'becoming' nature of this book itself. Even at this early stage (textually speaking) it is, in one sense, already written: the thinking has been done, content and themes organised, the structure planned. And yet there still remains the writing itself – without which this 'virtual' book (to borrow a fashionable idiom from the world of IT) will never actually exist. It will be there in potential, but will never have become what it essentially (within my own mind, at least) is.

Similarly we know this to be true of ourselves – equally paradoxically yet equally truly, and more fully in keeping with the context of Maurice's original statement – in our experience and understanding of Christian baptism. As it has been traditionally understood, and as it is still celebrated in our liturgy today, baptism 'does' a variety of things and effects a number of changes in the believer. Three of these in particular are of central importance to the understanding of the relationship between ontology and becoming. Thus the water of baptism proclaims through powerful symbol both the 'washing of regeneration' and the dying and rising of the believer with Christ, and with these two motifs must be coupled (in modern baptismal rites, at least) the idea of membership of, or incorporation into Christ's body, the church, expressed through the welcome into its fellowship in which the whole congregation joins.

All of these three things are proclaimed as being 'effected' by baptism: we are cleansed from sin, united with Christ in his risen life, and joined to the worldwide community of believers. And yet it is patently obvious that in each case there is a need for a lifelong realisation of that state – a continuous case of becoming what you are, without which the entire process is vitiated at source.

The paradox is intensified when we realise that baptism must be thus understood – on both a *de facto* and a becoming model at one and the same time. For if we take away the *de facto* element then baptism is nothing more than a pious hope and a set of broken promises – in the vast majority of cases at least. It must be an expression of what 'is', and is yet to become incarnate in this particular human life. This 'isness' of potential (to coin a phrase) must be complemented and completed by a lifetime of continual becoming, only at the end of which (and even then, only on the other side of death, and with it resurrection and new creation) will potential and reality become fully united.

At times during Christian history this process of becoming has been not merely present – as it surely must be – in the background of the spiritual life, but has (and in my view rightly) come into the foreground and provided a governing motif and model for Christian spirituality and devotion. One such period, which over the last generation or so has increasingly come back into fashion, is that of the classic expression of Celtic Christianity, covering the period, say, from the mid fifth century to the mid ninth century, and encompassing such figures as Patrick, Columba, Adomnan, Brendan the Navigator, Columbanus and many others. Admittedly there is something of a debate going on at present as to precisely how distinctive this period actually was, and attempting to distinguish what, if anything, is authentically Celtic from the accretions of myth and

romanticisation.[1] But even if one allows for some rigorous prun-
ing of the Celtic identity, certain ideas appear resolutely to
refuse to be banished. Central among these is the concept of pilgrimage. Essential to the Celtic understanding of pilgrimage is
the idea that a physical journey from one place to another is a
symbol – a physical acting out – of the spiritual and internal
journey which each of us makes throughout our lives. To go on a
pilgrimage is not just to journey from one place to another or to
perform some sort of 'one off' spiritual exercise, but to perform
an action integral to the spiritual life, and whose function is to
direct the gaze inwards to enable us all the better to recognise,
and if necessary re-orientate, the journey which is constantly
being enacted there.

With this primary focus established, then, the outward pilgrimage has two components – mirrored in the internal pilgrimage – the goal and the journey itself. The goal may be a holy
place, or it may be a quest to find one's 'place of resurrection', or
it may be, like Abraham's, a journey to an unknown destination:
the only certainty is that the final resting place is one in which
God is especially, and in some distinctive fashion, to be met, and
where he is undoubtedly already waiting for us. Alongside this
goal runs the journey itself, and for the Celtic mind and heart
God was there on the journey also, to be met with as the pilgrim
rejoiced in the manifold beauties of the way, or was protected
from dangers, or performed simple daily acts with prayer such
as rising and lying down. In all of this there is again to be seen
the paradox of a 'here and now' reality and a process of becoming or of realised potential. For a pilgrimage depends entirely –
in one sense at least – on its end or goal: if this is for some reason
not attained the pilgrimage remains incomplete and has failed
to achieve its object, and all that the pilgrim feels is a sense of
disappointment and perhaps even of failure. At the same time,
however, if the goal is achieved, then the process of getting there
assumes tremendous significance also, and the pilgrim will reflect on the many epiphanies and insights gained along the way,
and the wonders of the journey will stand in perfect balance
with the ultimate achievement of reaching the journey's end.
Ontological status and becoming are once again held in a creative, if at times paradoxical, tension.

This concept of becoming, then, is a foundational one for our own spiritual experience. It starts from a very different set of questions and premises than do the traditional distinctions of degree and kind christological thinking, but it is my contention that, if applied to Jesus and the relationship between his human identity and his divine status as the Christ, it opens up several fruitful and positive areas of thought about, and response to Jesus, some of which have echoes, although no more, of the kind of 'evolutionary' theology pioneered by the extraordinary French Jesuit thinker, Pierre Teilhard de Chardin. Similarly, although I would not wish to ally myself too closely with it, there may perhaps be links to be followed up between this kind of thinking and that branch of theology known as 'process theology'.

Whatever the links with other areas of theology may be, though, the concept of becoming is a pivotal one in this attempt to discover a new way of doing christology. It casts the Christship and Son-ship of Jesus in the context of realised potential, and by undercutting any suggestion of a fixed ontological state for Jesus (or indeed for anyone else) it opens up the possibility of movement and becoming from both a human and a divine standpoint. Specifically, it creates the potential for an organic (rather than any more mechanical or *a priori* understanding) realisation of incarnation in which humanity can aspire to divinity and divinity can assume a perfected humanity. The unity between Jesus and the Christ therefore becomes contingent upon a realised potential, rather than being necessary as the result of some given ontological arrangement and argument.

It should also be pointed out at this stage that although it flies in the face of many of the most venerable traditions of christology, this position is by no means inconsistent with the witness of scripture. Substantial (if surprising, given its usual interpretation) reference will be made in a later chapter to St John's gospel in the context of whether Jesus is necessarily and pre-existently the Christ; but for the present it is sufficient to note the all too frequently overlooked opening of St Paul's Epistle to the Romans:

> Paul, a servant of Jesus Christ, called to be an apostle, set apart for the gospel of God which he promised beforehand

through his prophets in the holy scripture, the gospel concerning his Son, who was descended from David according
to the flesh and designated Son of God in power according to
the spirit of holiness by his resurrection from the dead, Jesus
Christ our Lord ...

As always, Paul's prose is dense; but even if complicated, his
meaning is clear. He is unambiguous as to the full (and ordinary) humanity of Jesus – 'descended from David according to
the flesh' – suggesting that Joseph was the biological father of
Jesus, rather than side-stepping the issue simply by citing
Joseph as Mary's husband as Matthew's genealogy does. More
significantly even than this, Jesus' Sonship appears to be retrospective: Jesus is 'designated' the Son of God as the ultimate fulfilment of what I have called a 'realised potential'. This is a fact
noted with his usual acuity by Marcus J. Borg in his recent study
of Jesus: 'If we hear Paul's words without later Christian teaching affecting how we interpret them, they suggest that Jesus's
status as Son of God began at Easter.'[2] Clearly once this Sonship
has been 'designated' it casts a retrospective light of divinity
back over the whole life and ministry of Jesus, but that is not at
all the same thing as saying that this Sonship was there unalter-
ably and necessarily from the beginning. Things could (as
Gerald O'Collins reminded us earlier) have been different – and
this key possibility is only there if the unity between Jesus and
the Christ is contingent and not necessary.

With this reassuring proviso, then, that we are not departing
entirely from the possibilities contained within scripture itself,
my own christological convictions – and therefore those of this
book – begin from a foundational need to do full justice to the
total humanity at least as much as to the divinity of Jesus Christ.
It is my further conviction that traditional christology has never
been entirely successful in this regard, and given the difficulties
involved in operating within a framework of fixed ontological
identities, this is hardly surprising.

Admittedly it is hard for the human mind to conceive of a
satisfactory way in which humanity and divinity can co-inhere
equally in one individual, especially if the parameters are that
this co-inherence must be that of two ontologically different

entities which are arranged in perfect balance (whatever that might mean!) from the outset – indeed it is a little like trying to mix oil and water!

Furthermore, there is an almost inbuilt limitation – and therefore a potential source of problems – in this manner of thinking. This is simply the requirement that divinity will be in no way diminished (other than perhaps by a process of *kenosis* or self-emptying) through its association with humanity. Thus, in any traditional christological construction, the fullness of divinity must always be present in the man Jesus of Nazareth if he is also to be proclaimed as the Christ and the Son of God. It is this insistence on the present and completely realised fulfilment of Jesus' divinity from the very first moment of his human existence (as presented, for example, by the birth narratives of Matthew and Luke, in contrast to Mark, John and Paul who appear to know nothing of them) which has had, historically, a fatal tendency to skew the picture of Jesus. What has happened is that in any number of ways in different generations the humanity of Jesus (for all that there may have been very real attempts to stress it) has effectively and inevitably been subsumed in the divinity of the Christ. There is, throughout christological history, an implicit tendency towards Apollinarianism or even Docetism – although never, of course, within an orthodox framework, going so far as to rehabilitate either of these early heresies.

There is, as we have mentioned briefly above, an entirely laudable motive for this tendency, and this is simply the passionate desire to safeguard the perfection and 'completeness' of divinity even (and perhaps especially) as it meets humanity most intimately. That this desire should be a powerful dominating force in Christian theology from its earliest days is readily understandable. The history of the relationship between gods and human beings in the Graeco-Roman world was, on the whole, not a particularly illuminating or uplifting one. The gods had a regrettable tendency to behave in less than edifying or responsible ways (indeed frequently even in unethical ones) in their dealings with humanity, and one may well imagine that within that ancient world there would have been a strong wish, even from the very earliest days, to dissociate Christianity from such a thought world. Incarnation is, after all, something rather different from merely meddling with human lives and affairs.

Laudable and understandable it might well be, but this pre-eminent need to safeguard divinity from any prospect of pollution or diminution through its association with humanity led to a gradual distancing of the divine/human figure of Jesus Christ from any other manifestation of humanity whatsoever.

That this is so is arguably most evident in the assumptions (if that is the right word!) surrounding the primogeniture of Jesus and the status of his mother. Historically the earliest documents in the New Testament are almost certainly the epistles of St Paul (dating from the late 40s onwards), and the earliest gospel is generally felt (although the consensus is by no means unanimous) to be that of St Mark, which is usually held to date from sometime around the year 70AD. Interestingly, neither of these authors shows the slightest interest in – or even knowledge of – anything extraordinary about the birth or parentage of Jesus, and indeed, as we have seen, St Paul actually suggests that 'according to the flesh' Jesus had a perfectly ordinary human parentage: that of Mary and Joseph. The later gospels of St Matthew and St Luke – and increasingly afterwards the whole weight of Christian tradition – then focus on the uniqueness of Jesus' birth and parentage, stressing the virginity of Mary and the merely spousal and protector-oriented role (and not any biological one, which is indeed denied both implicitly and explicitly in these gospels) of Joseph in Jesus' fathering.

Given the probable relative dates of the various documents involved, it is hard to avoid the conclusion (unless one supposes, somewhat improbably, that Matthew and Luke had access to a tradition denied to both Paul and Mark) that these concerns with virginity and the lack of any human father for Jesus are later accretions to the original story. The underlying reasons for such accretions are not hard to discern: the uniqueness of Jesus as the Christ and with it the ontological perfection of divinity must be protected at all costs. And what a cost it has increasingly turned out to be! Here, at one stroke, Jesus is severed from the rest of humanity, a severance which the Roman Catholic Church in particular has intensified by means of two subsequent promulgations concerning not merely Jesus himself, but also his mother, such that at its most extreme the full humanity not only of Jesus but also of Mary appears to be under threat. We will deal with the later dogmas in due course, but it is to the relatively early doctrine of the Virgin Birth (or more properly the Virginal Conception) that we must first turn.

Initially, then, we may assume that the reasoning behind the inclusion of this element in the gospels of Matthew and Luke (and then in much early Christian teaching during the sub-apostolic era) was simply a desire to stress the 'specialness' – indeed the uniqueness – of the infant thus conceived and born: and indeed the idea of parthenogenesis as conferring particular status on an individual is not confined merely to Christianity in the religious myths of the ancient world. This by itself might have been assimilable as a picturesque, symbolic way of asserting the especial significance of Jesus, but what later (and entirely contrary to intention) vitiated any value which this might have had, was the 'rounding out' of this symbolism and the connection of it with ontology and morality which was supplied by generations of patristic theologians, most notably – and from the standpoint of this discussion, most destructively – by St Augustine of Hippo. More will be said of Augustine in a subsequent chapter, but his negative contribution must at least be noted here.

Others, admittedly, had paved the way before him, but it was Augustine who made more explicit perhaps than anyone else the supposed connection between sexual intercourse and original sin, and who defined original sin not merely as a propensity to sin, but as an ontological 'state' of innate sinfulness, and therefore also of guilt, transmitted from generation to generation by the process of procreation itself, and for which we stand in need of forgiveness and redemption even before we have drawn our first breath.

Believing such a picture of our human state to be true, clearly the saviour of the human race could not possibly be born under the same cloud of original sin as the rest of humankind, otherwise redemption becomes an exercise in hauling oneself upwards by one's own boot-straps. The symbolic power of the Virginal Conception is thereby transformed into an ontological necessity: here is the means by which Jesus can share our humanity and yet remain free of its taint.

A similar line of thought, although the doctrine was not

officially promulgated until the nineteenth century, lies behind
the Roman Catholic dogma of the Immaculate Conception.
What this does is to safeguard the perfection of Jesus by placing
the severance from original sin one generation further back with
his mother. As a dogma it represents little more than an entirely
illogical second line of defence for the purity of Jesus. It safeguards this purity by announcing that Mary herself was free
from original sin, and therefore (given the already established
Virginal Conception of Jesus) Jesus could not possibly have inherited this taint either 'genetically' or through the sexual intercourse of his parents. It is, however, entirely illogical, in that if
God could protect Mary from original sin in this way, then why
not Jesus – especially since Jesus had, as Mary did not, the added
protection of a virginal conception? And if Jesus could have been
spared original sin through an Immaculate (and Virginal)
Conception, then what is the logic behind the Immaculate
Conception of Mary? Doctrinally it is unnecessary; spiritually it
reinforces the separation of Jesus from 'normal' humanity.

Finally, there is the most recent Marian promulgation, that of
the Assumption of the Blessed Virgin Mary. The immediate relevance of this to the full humanity of Jesus is admittedly less obvious, but it is nonetheless real. For what this dogma does is to
place Jesus' mother, Mary, at one remove from the rest of humanity, and if she is thus distanced from us, it is well-nigh impossible to conceive of Jesus as being fully human in any entirely
meaningful way.

It should be stressed at this point that I have no quarrel with
the original intention behind any of these dogmatic positions:
the Virginal Conception of Jesus, the Immaculate Conception,
and the Assumption of the Blessed Virgin Mary – or even, indeed, with at least some form or another of a doctrine of original
sin, of which, owing to its especial significance, more in the next
chapter. It is natural and inevitable that any faith – Christianity
included – should wish to stress the particularity and specialness of its central figure, in this case, Jesus; and one way of doing
this is undoubtedly to highlight in pictorial, symbolic fashion,
the unique circumstances which, mythically at least, surround
the existence of that figure. However, what has happened historically is that symbol has become petrified into religious and

spiritual 'fact': Jesus was virginally conceived, and, for Roman Catholics at least, Mary really was immaculately conceived and assumed into heaven. And the consequences of this are disastrous: indeed they are not only disastrous but also deeply ironic, and the resulting complications for Christianity would be almost laughable if they had not also proved so painful, restrictive and destructive for generation after generation of Christian believers.

The disaster lies in the fact that these various dogmas, designed principally to reinforce the uniqueness of Jesus (and therefore his exalted place as redeemer and saviour) succeed only too well, and Jesus is no longer meaningfully 'one of us'. Indeed, viewed through this particular series of filters which remove all trace of sexuality from his conception and every potential for (let alone the reality of) sin, it is hard to see how Jesus can still be described as recognisably human at all.

And herein lies the irony! An ontological difference has been opened up (whether we recognise it as such or phrase it in precisely these terms or not) between Jesus and ourselves, and we find ourselves separated from our supposedly human saviour by two of the very things which, amongst others no doubt, constitute our distinctive humanity: our potential for sin, and our possession of a distinct and powerful sexuality which has led to the genesis of every member (save one, according to the traditional argument!) of the human race.

The result of this is not only a separation from our saviour, but a fear of precisely those things which separate us, especially sexuality – of which more in Part Two of this study; and this, I would argue, has led throughout the ages to a consistent impoverishment not only of our individual human lives, but also of our church life and our spirituality and prayer, both corporate and private.

Is there, then, another way of approaching christology, or are we firmly stuck with the categories and problems with which twenty centuries of christological thinking have left us? Certainly there is a pressing need to attempt to find such a new approach, both because of the 'internal' difficulties described above, and also because of the fact, which we noted in the Introduction, that the traditional approach with its fixed ontology and broadly 'from above' orientation no longer engages with the mind-set and thought world of the vast bulk of humanity, and Jesus Christ is therefore removed even further from the possibility of interaction with the reality of human life.

This need to revisit and largely re-envision and reconstruct christology, and with it also much of Christianity – together with the depressing fact that the church and its theologians have generally shirked the task – was expressed with characteristic forcefulness a few years ago by no less a figure than John Bowden in a radio broadcast to commemorate the thirtieth anniversary of the publication of *Honest to God*, the text of which broadcast was later incorporated into a book, *Thirty Years of Honesty*. John Bowden writes so clearly that substantial quotation is appropriate:

> ... there are virtually no new substantial and intellectually attractive statements of traditional Christian belief which counter successfully the now well-established criticisms of it. But equally, it is proving virtually impossible for new insights to make their way. What we seem to have is either apathy or deliberate disregard of the many unanswered questions about Christianity, with little attempt to push through them and face the consequences ...
>
> That won't do. For it's abundantly clear that there is no way of putting together the pieces in which Christianity is now so that they add up to the old answers in some miraculously new form, and can provide justification for the churches as they are today ...
>
> Many people are still prepared to be interested in fundamental questions like the existence of God, the person of Jesus of Nazareth, the basis of morality, not to mention the very nature of language and all the issues raised by 'postmodernism'. But are the churches? There is very little evidence that they are. All the signs are that they are concerned above all with the routine of 'business as usual', 'proclaiming the gospel', being the churches as they have been.
>
> But on what basis? No-one would deny the need for their activities in areas of social, pastoral, national and international concern, but that is not the prime *raison d'être* of the

churches. Their credentials are a belief which must be put over, lived out and shown to be true in dialogue with the outside world. All down history they have been engaged in that dialogue in the intellectual and cultural situation of their time. What happens if they give it up now, as so clearly seems to be happening? Without a coherent intellectual foundation, what defence is there to the charge that much Christian teaching is brainwashing and indoctrination and that in ethos Christianity has become just one more ideology – a closed society run along lines laid down by those who choose to belong to it?

The problems have proved far greater than John Robinson ever envisaged, but at least he was on the right track. That is why, for me, *Honest to God*, warts and all, is something which shouldn't be forgotten. The quest for truth and integrity within the churches, both individual and corporate, still needs to be carried on, even if there is no knowing where it will lead.[3]

There may well be 'no knowing where it will lead', but the realm of christology (as Bowden himself implies) is surely a crucial area in which the process he describes needs to be undertaken, both because it is central to Christian faith itself, and also because the Jesus who stands at the heart of that faith must be, in each generation, interpreted coherently to the contemporary world if that faith is to be effective in public worship, in personal spirituality, in pastoral care, and in mission. To undertake this re-visioning may be alarming, even frightening, for some, but it is nonetheless necessary; and it is, I believe, only frightening if we lack confidence in the underlying robustness of our faith. As Dorothy L. Sayers put it almost seventy years ago:

It is right that ... [doctrines] should be pulled about and subjected to the most searching kind of enquiry. If the structure is truly knit, it will stand any strain, and prove its truth by its toughness. Pious worshippers, whether of mortal or immortal artists, do their deities little honour by treating their incarnations as something too sacred for rough handling; they only succeed in betraying a fear lest the structure should prove flimsy or false.[4]

Not only is it necessary and must be approached without an inappropriate fear, but I believe that a new approach can be found which avoids many of the difficulties highlighted earlier in this chapter, and which does full justice to humanity as much as to divinity in the Incarnation. Such an approach hinges on the concept of 'realised potential' to which we have already briefly alluded, and it will be my contention that approaching christology through this concept not only avoids several pitfalls, but also opens up a variety of interesting and creative perspectives not merely on christology itself, but also on ecclesiology, missiology, ecumenism and morality. Indeed, it enables (and requires) us to subject almost every area of Christian doctrine and practice to a scrutiny which may be at once fascinating and liberating. And it does so, as has been indicated implicitly already, by approaching the figure of Jesus Christ with a subtly different initial premise (and question) from that which any more traditional christological thinking has employed.

For most christologies the question to be answered has been, effectively, 'How is Jesus the Christ?' – a metaphysical question which demands a metaphysical, and therefore abstract, answer. For us, by contrast, the question may well be expressed as being, 'How did Jesus become the Christ?' – a question of being and becoming which throws us not into a world of abstractions, but back to the concrete, compelling and often uncomfortable figure of Jesus of Nazareth, with whom, if he is indeed to be called Christ, christology must in some sense begin.

Before we can presume to answer this question, however, we must first proceed to lay a theological ghost and slay a metaphysical dragon! First, then, we must re-visit, at least briefly, the world of original sin and St Augustine, and establish how a christology of becoming may be at all compatible with any notion of original sin. To establish this satisfactorily is essential before proceeding any further, first, because this doctrine provides potentially the biggest single stumbling-block for any christology of becoming, and secondly because if we would remain within even the broadest bounds of orthodoxy then this doctrine must be at least creatively re-interpreted, rather than simply ignored, abandoned or conveniently glossed over.

Secondly, then, we must cast the net wider than simply

Augustine and his thought forms, and explore the worlds of
metaphysics and ontology, and in particular the way in which,
under the influence of philosophy, theology has been held in
thrall, first to the categories of Greek and Latin metaphysics,
secondly to a philosophical dream of the supremacy of ontology
over theology, and thirdly and linked in to both of these, to the
Enlightenment conviction of the supremacy of reason and the
consequent emergence of the God of the philosophers as opposed to the God of the theologians and the faithful. Recent de-
velopments in theology and philosophy have challenged these
positions, and as this work is founded upon an undermining of
much of traditional metaphysics and ontology, it is important to
establish that the christological innovation envisaged here is
fully consonant with much of the work which is going on in
other fields of Christian theology at the present time. But first, to
the spectre of St Augustine and original sin.

Notes
1. See especially, Oliver Davies and Fiona Bowie, *Celtic Christian
Spirituality: An Anthology of Medieval and Modern Sources*, London,
SPCK, 1995.
2. Marcus J. Borg, *Jesus: Uncovering the Life, Teachings and Relevance of a
Religious Revolutionary*, London, SPCK, 2011, p 66 (First pub. in USA
2006).
3. John Bowden, 'A Loss of Nerve', in *Thirty Years of Honesty: Honest to
God Then and Now*, ed John Bowden, London, SCM Press, 1993, pp 74-
83, (pp 82-83).
4. Dorothy L. Sayers, *The Mind of the Maker*, London, Methuen, 1941, p 74.

CHAPTER TWO

Guilty or Not Guilty

Theology is, even to those working within it – and almost cert-ainly so to those outside it – a curious discipline. At one level it appears to be attempting to do the impossible: to speak of the in-effable and the infinite from within the compass of finite human thought and speech. As such it is thereby diffuse, provisional, ever open to new possibilities and categories of thought. At an-other level, it is altogether harder-edged and more clear cut, and its own internal structures reveal that it is not called *theo-logy* for nothing. There is an underlying fundamental logic which gov-erns the relationship between its various parts, and what is said in the context of one doctrine can only possibly be acceptable if it is shown to be consonant with – or at least not directly con-trary to – that which needs to be said in the context of another doctrine.

Lest this sound too abstract, an example will readily clarify the truth of this. Thus all varieties of the penal substitution theory of the atonement are found, by this method, ultimately to be flawed. For we need to be able to say, on the one hand, that God is a God of (among other things) love, grace, mercy, forgiveness and so on, and it stands in direct contradiction to these qualities if we insist also that God required a sacrifice and had to punish someone in order for this forgiveness to be brought about. The two pictures of God are flatly incompatible (notwithstanding a variety of valiant medieval efforts to argue otherwise), and you can only consistently argue for a penal substitution atonement theory if you first argue for a very different primary conception of God from the one which Christianity has always claimed to worship.

It is this requirement to adhere to the internal logic of theology which brings us to the need for this particular chapter before we can proceed to outline a christology of becoming in any more detail. Quite simply, if the Augustine-governed traditional view of sin is correct, then there is no possible starting-point for such a christology as I have in mind, and we are thrown back to needing all of the safeguards – however inadequate and distancing of our Saviour they may be – of virginal conception and so on, in order to ensure that the supposedly sinless one could indeed have been sinless. For if St Augustine was right, then a naturally conceived Jesus would have been 'one of us' in all too literal a sense, including being up to his neck in original sin as mapped out by Augustine, and from such a beginning there is no way available of becoming the Christ, since perfection is, according to this schema, by definition, impossible.

So it is essential that we explore here both what this doctrine says, and also why it says what it does, and then consider further two things: its own internal cohesiveness and its scriptural warrant, before deciding whether it must stand for all time, or is, alternatively, open to modification or even rejection.

Augustine himself is uncompromising, and Christianity has, on the whole, followed his lead. His view is clear cut:

> … those who are not by this means [that is, grace] set free … are certainly righteously condemned, since they are not without sin, either that which they derived from their birth or that which they added by their evil lives.
>
> Therefore the whole 'lump' is under an obligation to suffer punishment …[1]

He is equally forthright in his views when condemning those who believe differently, and are therefore in his view heretics – in this case the Pelagians:

> They also deny that infants, born according to Adam after the flesh, contract by their first (i.e. natural) birth the infection of the ancient death … The reason why they are baptised is that by their New Birth they may be adopted and admitted into the kingdom of God, carried from good to better – not, by that renewal, delivered from any evil of ancient entail.[2]

Humanity is tainted from birth (indeed from conception) by participation in the sin of Adam, and also, equally importantly, by participation in his guilt. Sin and guilt are passed on simply by the act of procreation, and there is no escape from its shadow: it is a depressing but defining part of the human condition and a major aspect of the need for redemption – at least as important as those sins which we commit independently as individuals. To be human is to be sinful: it is (as with the categories discussed in the Introduction and Chapter 1) a *de facto* ontological state.

In the face of this regrettable situation, there are, it seems, two separate questions to be asked and answered. The first is why the church should so consistently have upheld Augustine's basic position, and never, since Pelagius, seriously questioned it; and the second is how and why Augustine arrived at this view-point in the first place.

The answer to the first of these questions is necessarily spec-ulative, since the church keeps no record of why it upholds cer-tain things; and this speculation brings me back, curiously and unexpectedly, to the central premise of a previous and very dif-ferent book. This book is *The Seeking Church: A Space for All,* and the central premise is that the church has been, for the entirety of its history, what I have come to describe as a 'Dispensing Church' – that is, a church which claims to have (or even asserts that it knows that it has) the full repository of truth, which it is ready and willing to give out to faithful and obedient believers.

To a church of this kind, the attractions of developing such a neat and tidy clear-cut doctrine as Augustine's are obvious. It is one among many of the Dispensing Church's ideal tools of con-trol. Thus, for certainly the larger part of its history, the church has had a relatively uneducated (and often largely illiterate) membership, and it is hard to imagine a better means of secur-ing conformity than by informing everyone that, regardless of their own personal lifestyle, they are destined for perdition (graphically described, and even sometimes painted on the walls of churches, to reinforce the message) unless they embrace the salvation which only the church is empowered by God to offer. Small wonder then, that in, for example, the flux of the Reformation, as new churches struggled to birth, all the reform-ers, without exception, placed such stress on innate human sin-fulness – what better way to establish the credentials of an infant church than by showing it to be the means of salvation not mere-ly from personal sin (which might, however mendaciously, be denied) but from the human condition of sinfulness itself. That this perception of the church as being intimately concerned with issues of power and control is widespread, and not merely a product of my own imagination, is borne out by its appearance, not only in theological writings, but even in popular fiction as, for example, Donna Leon's novel *The Girl of His Dreams*: '… as a group clerics are best avoided … It's their interest in power … that makes me so dislike them: so many of them are driven by it. I think it distorts their souls.'[3] Original sin is a valuable weapon in the attempt to exercise such power!

Admittedly it is to take speculation a little further – and the issue cannot be proved – but the consistency with which the church has upheld Augustine on this matter suggests strongly that dominance and control were at least as important in the Pelagian controversy as were matters more strictly theological. Pelagius' clash with Augustine was primarily over the issue of free will, but one can most certainly sense the spectre of original sin lurking, as we have seen in the quotation from *De Haeresibus* above – happily for Augustine and fatefully for Pelagius – in the background. Pelagius had had the temerity to suggest that human will was genuinely free – free to choose the good, and to respond in complete and purely human freedom to the goodness of its creator. In other words, there was, ultimately, a human capability for perfection: never realised, perhaps, but genuinely there in principle.

Not so, as we have seen, for Augustine. For him the only human route to goodness was through the prevenient grace of God. Without this the innate human condition of sinfulness (meaning, effectively, original sin as a *de facto* ontological given), weighed the scales so heavily that freely chosen goodness was an impossibility. Only grace would save the day, and without it humanity was locked into its own destruction. History records all too brutally the outcome of this controversy. The rumour of innate human goodness has hardly dared to show its face in respectable theological circles from that day to this, and the church has enjoyed the power which has resulted from being the divinely appointed channel of that grace which is the only way to re-direct and redeem this fallen human will.

If the question of why the church has chosen to collude with

Augustine for something like 1,600 years is relatively straight-forward (if unflattering to it) to answer, then the question of how and why Augustine originally reached his conclusions is altogether more complex, involving issues both of historical perspective and of personal psychology and worldview.

To begin with Augustine himself: he was, to put it mildly, a complex personality, and, as far as one can tell, a troubled one. Even if one had the necessary qualifications there would be little point in attempting any kind of post-mortem psychoanalysis of Augustine, but whatever the inner workings of his psyche may have been, it is certain that he held very particular – and extreme – views on the subject of human sexuality. I have discussed this already in a previous book,[4] but it is necessary for the sake of the clarity of our argument, to revisit this same territory at least briefly here.

Augustine's life, then, perhaps almost more so than anybody else's (with, though for entirely different reasons, the possible exception of St Paul's), can be divided into two drastically different sections: pre- and post-conversion. Prior to his conversion to Christianity Augustine had been a man of powerful and passionate sexuality, keeping a concubine for a number of years (much to the distress of his Christian mother, Monica) and fathering a child by her. On conversion every vestige of his former life – and with it all traces of overt sexuality – were pushed away. There was no question of marriage and a Christian hallowing of this relationship. Instead the whole of his former life was interpreted by Augustine as being almost unmitigatedly evil, and was therefore to be henceforth entirely repudiated. Concubine and child were set aside, and human sexuality was henceforward viewed as being intimately connected with the well-springs of human sinfulness.

Having developed, upon conversion, this polarised attitude towards his own life, is it in any way too fanciful to suggest that Augustine's own experience later coloured his own developed theological opinions? Seeing his own sexual life as being 'sunk in sin', it is small wonder that he came to regard sexual activity as being the transmitter of such sin (and with it guilt) through the act of procreation. One might almost say that Augustine's perception of his own state of sin was then imputed (or projected) by him on to every other member of the human race.

By whatever means Augustine reached his conclusions, however – and while we may well want to question the objective soundness of the reasoning which led him in that direction – there still remains the critical question of whether or not he was necessarily right. Did his somewhat dubious premises yet somehow lead him to some appropriate conclusions?

To answer this question we must, I think, return to Augustine's (and our) primary data; that is, scripture, and assess whether Augustine's presentation of sin and guilt is necessarily found there, or whether, in fact, his own pre-occupation with human sin has led him to extrapolate from it more than the scriptural narrative itself actually warrants.

What, in fact, transpires if we examine the story of the Fall in some detail is that Augustine's interpretation is found to be not the only possible interpretation, and indeed, by no means the one most consonant with the thrust of the narrative itself.

So what does the story have to tell us, in mythic form admittedly, about the state of humanity? It states first, in unequivocal terms, that humanity, in the form of Adam and Eve, was created in a state of goodness: God, we are told, saw that it was 'very good'.

And if we then follow through the story (or more properly stories, since there are, in fact, two of them) recorded in Genesis, what do we find, and what, therefore, should our theological conclusions be? The truth of the matter is that what we actually find contained within the story itself is very different from that which St Augustine reads into it and imputes to it. Certainly we see a story which, in mythical form, delineates the human race's perennial susceptibility to sin, and we may even allow that, again through the medium of myth, it links sin with the whole condition of human temporality and mortality. What we most emphatically do not find is any suggestion that a condition of sin – and most particularly its associated guilt – is transmitted from generation to generation by the simple process of procreation. It is fair to say that the Bible knows nothing of the doctrine of original sin in its full-blown Augustinian manifestation.

Such has long been my conviction, and it has therefore been heartening of late to find a champion of this position in one of the most distinguished Roman Catholic theologians of the present generation, James P. Mackey. In recent years Mackey has written two books of particular significance as far as this topic is concerned: one an academic systematic theology, and the other a more reflective and meditative study of the life of Jesus, and in both of them he is adamant that Christianity has suffered grievously from St Augustine's entirely negative perception of humanity.

Mackey is quite clear that Augustine's doctrine is thoroughly unbiblical:

> No … biblical text or context contain[s] such an inherently questionable concept as that of the transmission of sin or penalty by the very process of generation, and that presumably by divine decree.[5]

Or again he argues that the biblical story:

> … has nothing whatever to do with a theology of original sin that talks of an actual sin committed by our first parents and that is then transmitted to all later members of *homo sapiens* by the mere act of procreation, a scenario found nowhere in the Bible.[6]

What Mackey sees, and it is a vision of events with which I entirely concur, is a gradual process of separation from biblical roots during the first four centuries, which then reached its extreme position in St Augustine:

> … the only generalisation permissible to anyone who looks back to these remote origins of the Christian theology of the Fall is that it gradually lost the best of its biblical bearings, until it finally lost the plot altogether in that feature of the Fall that is traceable to Augustine and solemnly defined by the Roman Catholic Council of Trent in the sixteenth century. The feature, namely, that sees the original sin transmitted to every member of the human race, through the very process of their generation into that same human race.[7]

By way of summation, Mackey is trenchant in his condemnation of Augustine's doctrine:

> Augustine somehow managed to construct … the most disastrous doctrine of the Fall and original sin in the whole history of Christianity down to the present day.[8]

Augustine's presentation of original sin and guilt is thereby reduced to tatters and shown to be at once unbiblical and pernicious. But there is yet one more nail to be driven into the coffin of
Augustine's theology, and that is, quite simply, that Augustine
was necessarily a pre-critical reader of scripture, and like all
readers of his time simply assumed that the story of Adam and
Eve was historically accurate and referred to two specific
human beings who were indeed created directly by the hand of
God as depicted in the opening chapters of Genesis. To the post-
critical reader, however, it is plain that the story is cast in mythical form and is attempting to speak in pictorial mode of human
nature, and is not intended to refer to the deeds of any two specific people. Quite simply, Adam and Eve (from whom, according to Augustine, we inherit original sin and guilt) never existed, and however grievous their mythical sin may be deemed to
be, Augustine's theory of transmission becomes equally mythical. Just like Adam and Eve, it does not exist and never has existed.

If Augustine's theory, then, is both unworkable, unbiblical,
and ultimately unintelligible, with what may we justifiably replace it, based on the evidence of scripture and our own understanding and experience of human nature? If we are not to jetti-
son the concept of original sin altogether, how may it more reasonably and more theologically constructively be defined?

What the evidence of the story itself allows us to say is certainly that humanity is in some sense 'fallen'; but what it does
not allow us to superimpose onto this is the innate sinfulness
and especially guilt of all humanity. The human race is fallen in
the sense that every member of it is capable of – and even prone
to – sin, but this is an entirely different thing from asserting that
a state of *de facto* sinfulness and guilt is transmitted from generation to generation as the ultimate (and archetypical) sexually
transmitted disease! Original sin is thus simply, and no more
and no less than, the fact of our being creatures who are subject
to temptation and capable – indeed from time to time even likely
to do so – of succumbing to it. But it is not in itself a state of innate sinfulness prior to any act of our own, and certainly not a
condition of innate and inherited guilt.

If the doctrine of original sin is thus correctly defined and

stripped of all of St Augustine's negative and destructive accretions, we may then, with a good theological conscience, be perfectly content to retain this doctrine as a meaningful component
of our Christian theology – and it is, of course, also entirely consonant with our everyday experience of being human and
falling, more or less often as the case may be, into sin.

At this point, then, we may profitably return to the figure of
Jesus, and establish the reality of his relationship to this doctrine,
and discover that this may be very different from that which has
traditionally been supposed. All traditional christological thinking, then, has by and large assumed the Augustinian framework,
and clearly from within this framework there is a vital need to
distance Jesus from this aspect of the human condition, hence the
doctrines of the Virgin Birth, the Immaculate Conception and so
on. The Son of God cannot possibly be held to be tainted with the
corporate sin and inherited guilt of the rest of the human race: he
must, from this point of view at least, be different from us in kind
and not merely in degree.

Once set free from its Augustinian shackles, though, the doctrine of original sin poses no such problems, and may indeed
lend itself creatively to a theology of Jesus becoming the Christ.
For in this revised and, as we have argued, actually more biblical form, the doctrine speaks of the human propensity to sin in
terms of specific sinful actions, rather than of a straightforward
and universal human condition of sin and concomitant guilt
simply by virtue of being born.

According to this understanding of the doctrine, every
human being is born personally sinless, and the term 'original
sin' refers only to the potential for actual sin which is inherent in
every human being. Thus understood, we can begin to see the
life of Jesus as one which was indeed lived in this condition, and
which yet succeeded in transcending all temptation and retain-
ing to the end that initial state of sinlessness.

Such an understanding is compatible with, and I would suggest, even demanded by, the biblical accounts of Jesus' life.
Thus, for example, the synoptic gospels record the temptation of
Jesus in the wilderness at the outset of his ministry, and although these are stylised accounts they at least acknowledge the
reality of temptation in Jesus' earthly life. And unless we are

effectively to invalidate the fullness of Jesus' humanity we must accept the fact that the rejection of these temptations – that is, real temptations throughout Jesus' life, rather than merely these stylised wilderness temptations – was not a foregone or necessary conclusion. Jesus, being fully human, could have sinned. Admittedly he would not then have become the Christ, but that is entirely in keeping with the central thesis of this book, that becoming the Christ depended not on a necessary and fixed ontology, but upon a lifelong and voluntary 'Yes' to God.

With this understanding, then, we can retain the doctrine of original sin and fully accept the fact that the sinless one was born fully human and knowing – as being subject to temptation – the full force of original sin. For what this revised form of the doctrine does not do – which Augustine's version most emphatically does – is to deny the possibility of personal sinlessness. Original sin – shorn of Augustinianism – and actual personal sinlessness are perfectly compatible, and we may coherently argue that in becoming the Christ this is precisely the achievement – dependent upon contingent willing rather than necessary ontological status – of Jesus of Nazareth. With the spectre of St Augustine safely disposed of, we may now turn to the dragons of ontology and philosophy.

Notes

1. Augustine of Hippo, *de Natura at Gratia*, iv.4-v.5, quoted in *Creeds, Councils and Controversies*, ed J. Stevenson, London, SPCK, 1966, Sixth Impression 1981, pp 222-3.
2. Augustine of Hippo, *De Haerisibus*, 88, quoted in Stevenson, op. cit., p 225.
3. Donna Leon, *The Girl of His Deams*, London, Heinemann, 2008, p 44.
4. See, Stephen R. White, *The Right True End of Love*, Dublin, Columba Press, 2005, especially Chapter 4: 'Eros and Agape'.
5. James P. Mackey, *Christianity and Creation: The Essence of the Christian Faith and Its Future among Religions*, London, Continuum, 2006, p 75.
6. James P. Mackey, *Jesus of Nazareth: The Life, the Faith and the Future of the Prophet (A Brief History)*, Dublin, Columba Press, 2008, p 211.
7. Mackey, *Christianity and Creation*, pp 88-9.
8. Mackey, *Christianity and Creation*, p 91.

CHAPTER THREE

Theology: Enslaved or Free?

As an individual, St Augustine may have succeeded in exercising a stranglehold over certain areas of Christian doctrine for something over 1,600 years, but he is by no means alone in seeking to bind theology within certain narrow and pre-defined limits. It will therefore be the purpose of this chapter to identify three distinct but related movements or categories of thought which have sought to limit theology, and which have, indeed, all too often succeeded in doing so. For theology to be the kind of theology for which we saw John Bowden longing in Chapter One, it must learn to break free from these external constraints and develop its own freedom to create new premises and categories of thought – of which the concept of Christly becoming might stand as a prime example.

I do not propose to examine these three areas in a strictly chronological order, but rather, in what seems to me to be a more satisfactory logical order, beginning with the epoch which has cast its darkling shadow over the realm of theology for most of the last three hundred or so years – the Enlightenment.

This great intellectual age of the seventeenth and eighteenth centuries achieved many things and encompassed a myriad discoveries and advances, scientific, intellectual, practical and social. Ironically, however, its central project threatened (and largely succeeded in so doing) to strike at the very heart of the society which spawned it – that is, at its religious beliefs.

This central project was none other than the exaltation – indeed, well-nigh the deification – of human reason. There was to be nothing which was not susceptible to reason, and reason would unlock the truths both of the universe and of humanity within it. God was no longer logically or affectively necessary as an explanation for anything, and if it was necessary to acknowledge his existence at all any longer, then it was, essentially, only as another object to be known and classified. The living God of the Bible was eviscerated by the Enlightenment, and, for many, only a pale Deist shadow remained.

The impact of this was the birth – or re-birth, since Tertullian appears to have faced something of the same problem with his celebrated rhetorical question, 'What has Athens to do with Jerusalem?'[1] – of the God of the philosophers rather than the God of religion, faith, theology and worship. The problems which this poses for theology, and the fact that theology in large measure collaborated in creating its own difficulties, is brilliantly sketched out by John D. Caputo and Michael J. Scanlon:

> The claim of Descartes was that it is the proper task of philosophy, not theology, to investigate the questions of God and the soul. It seems that this claim went unchallenged at the time, since theology itself was content with a basically philosophical approach to its *praeambula fidei*. Philosophical or 'natural' theology even became a required course in the curricula of Roman Catholic seminaries both as a philosophy course and as the first theology course, *De Deo Uno*. Pascal's was a rather lonely voice in preference for the 'God of Abraham, Isaac, and Jacob' over the 'god of the philosophers'. Theologians came to prefer what seemed to them to be the far more rigorously rational (and, therefore, true) philosophical God, than the homiletically more attractive (but not quite true) anthropomorphic portrayals of the biblical God.[2]

The ramifications of this process of, to all intents and purposes, distilling God into nothing more than another category of thought to be assimilated and classified by human reason, have been immense and cumulatively destructive of both theology and faith. From it flows Arnold's 'long, melancholy, withdrawing roar' of the receding 'Sea of Faith' and the whole nineteenth century crisis of doubt, Nietzsche's announcement of the 'death of God' (which, as Phillip Blond acutely notes, is 'not a rejection of the God of the theologians, but that of the philosophers'[3]), and the sceptical and nihilistic undercurrent of so much of twentieth century life and thought.

And so to the present day, and to theology's pressing need to

break free from the religiously corrosive and spiritually hubris-
tic legacy of the Enlightenment. Happily there are signs that this
has begun to happen. Indeed, it could be said to have begun to
happen, albeit at the time almost unnoticed, several decades
ago. As long ago as 1941 Dorothy L. Sayers (best known as a
novelist and playwright, but no mean theologian either) commented with an almost uncanny prescience:

> We have begun to suspect that the purely analytical ap-
> proach to phenomena is only leading us further and further
> into the abyss of disintegration and randomness, and that it
> is becoming urgently necessary to construct a synthesis of
> life.[4]

Caputo and Scanlon, cited above, organised a conference at
Villanova University, Pennsylvania, in September 1997, under
the title of 'Religion and Postmodernism', the purpose of which
was to explore ways in which that nexus of ideas, concepts and
methods understood as Postmodernism (Derrida was a key
speaker), might facilitate a movement away from an Enlightenment strait-jacket. In their introduction to the book of papers
which stemmed from this conference, *God, the Gift, and Postmodernism*, they deftly outline their hopes for the conference and
for the emergence of an authentic religious voice. It is deserving
of extensive quotation:

> Our interest, in particular, was to examine the evasive man-
> oeuvres and overcomings that have been undertaken with
> regard to the axioms and certainties of the Enlightenment in
> the last quarter of this century, precisely insofar as that work
> has resulted in a discourse which is more congenial to reli-
> gion. Let us suppose that the inaugural and constituting act
> of modernity in the seventeenth century was an act of exclus-
> ion or bracketing; that the modern epoch turns on an *epoche*, a
> methodological imperative, in which modernity made up its
> mind to abide by human reason alone. In the *via moderna*, the
> rule will be that we are to make our way along a way ... illu-
> minated by the light of reason alone, of what was called rea-
> son in the seventeenth and eighteenth century. If that is so,
> then one way to think of the effect we were trying to provoke

in this conference is to imagine its participants as engaged in the common pursuit of pushing past the constraints of this old, methodologically constricted, less enlightened, strait and narrow Enlightenment, which found it necessary to cast 'reason' and 'religion' in mortal opposition. We sought to seize the contemporary moment which has loosened the grip of the old Enlightenment, questioned its intimidating authority, complained about the exclusionary force of its certainties and axioms (among which secularism has enjoyed pride of place), and thereby made some room for a religious discourse and restored the voice of a religious imagination, the Enlightenment, as Derrida said of Marx, having chased away one ghost too many. Our wager was, the more enlightened we get about Enlightenment, the more likely religion is to get a word in edgewise.[5]

Such a stance, of deliberately attempting to create a backlash against the Enlightenment is theologically heartening, and lends a welcome momentum to this book's attempt to do theology on theology's own terms, and not in fiefdom to any externally imposed framework of categories or supposed truths.

For our second and third areas for consideration we must jump first backwards and then forwards in time from the Enlightenment, in order to consider first a development which has left theology permanently a prey to philosophy, and secondly a specific legacy of the Enlightenment which has had profound theological consequences and which has only recently begun to be seriously challenged.

Looking backwards first, then, let us return to Tertullian's famous question, 'What has Athens to do with Jerusalem?' for, with no doubt the very best of intentions, theology sowed the seeds of its future philosophical slavery by its insistence on relocating the God of Israel to Greece.

Thus the centuries of the patristic era represented a gradual process of systematisation, as the God of the Bible was explored, explained and defined using the categories of Greek (and Latin) metaphysics. Laudable in intention it may have been, but one may nonetheless question whether it was not a monumental derailing of the faith of the early church. One can see why the

intelligentsia of the Roman Empire wanted to translate the materials of faith into the common philosophical currency of the
day, but at the same time, from the point of view of the dy-
namism of that faith, one can question the ultimate wisdom of
the project, for it changed radically from that day to this the
whole understanding of the theological task.

For we should not be mistaken: this was not the invention of
theology, but rather its transformation into something far removed from its origins, and remote from the world of the Bible.
For there had been theology before, and the Bible is full of it in
both the Old and the New Testaments, but it is a radically different form of theology from that which came to birth during the
patristic centuries. Thus the theology of the Bible is what might
be called a theology of activity, a theology of doing. The Old
Testament is a galvanising and fast-paced record of Israel's
changing perception of its relationship with God, based on what
are perceived as God's acts to reward, safeguard or punish his
chosen people. And even those parts of the Old Testament
which are most overtly introspective dwell more on the activity
of God than on any more abstract speculation about his nature
in himself. So, for example, in the midst of his manifold tribula-
tions the major question on Job's mind (and also on the minds of
his 'comforters') is not, 'What kind of a God does these things?'
but rather, 'Why has God brought me such misfortune?'
Similarly, the mythical figure of Jonah remonstrates with God
towards the end of his story, complaining not about the niceties
of God's metaphysical being, but about his knowledge of how
God chooses to act: '… I knew that you are a gracious God and
merciful, slow to anger, and abounding in steadfast love, and
ready to relent from punishing' (4:2).

Conversely, if this is true of theology which relates to God
himself, it is equally true of what might be called the practical
theology of response – in other words, what God demands of his
people. And this is seen, time and again, to be not the minutiae of
correct belief, but a right orientation to God and a right daily
praxis; a position perhaps best summed up by the prophet
Micah: 'He has told you, O mortal, what is good; and what does
the Lord require of you but to do justice, and to love kindness,
and to walk humbly with your God' (6:8).

In terms of theological method, there is little change if we move forward to the New Testament. Looking first at the gospels, the whole tenor of Jesus' teaching is oriented towards how his disciples are to live, rather than towards what, precisely, they are to believe. And this teaching is, appropriately, rooted in what we might call a practical rather than a metaphysical or ontologically dominated theology. In the parables, for example, God, or concepts such as the kingdom of heaven are invoked and alluded to (though never with any claim to a one-on-one representational accuracy) and aspects of them sketched by means of word pictures: the kingdom of heaven 'may be likened to' a mustard seed or a pearl of great price; God, similarly may be likened to (but never equated with) a generous employer, the father of the Prodigal Son and so on. In such stories there is a definite theology at work, but as in the Old Testament it is primarily a theology of activity rather than being, in that its central thrust is that the disciples are to live lives of compassion and self-giving because in so doing they will reflect the nature, will and activity of God himself.

This sense of a practical rather than a more abstract theology remains true even if we turn from the faster paced and action-driven synoptic gospels to the more poetic and reflective gospel according to St John. This, of all the gospels, is the most overtly theological, but even here the theology is, as it were, applied rather than purely conceptual or theoretical. Thus, for example, John's Jesus, in the long discourse which encompasses the bulk of chapters fourteen to seventeen, returns continually to the theme of the oneness of the Father and the Son, and indeed, in chapter fourteen especially, of the Holy Spirit also. On the face of things, this might look like the perfect opportunity for a lengthy excursus into a dominical lecture on metaphysics. But this is emphatically not the case. For in this discourse Jesus is far more concerned simply to emphasise the fact of his oneness with the Father and to draw out its implications for the oneness of the disciples also, than he is to pick over the metaphysical niceties of precisely how this oneness might exist ontologically.

For all of the theology contained within them, however, the gospels, that of St John included, are primarily narratives and not theological meditations, and we might therefore expect to find a more abstract theologising when we turn to the epistles, especially those of St Paul, for these, after all, although written earlier than the gospels themselves, are attempts to explore and explain to the young churches the meaning of the events which would come to be recounted in those gospels. But again this proves to be not so. For St Paul, theology is not an intellectual game to be played for its own sake, but a practical tool in the service of church life and both personal and corporate ethics. As I wrote some ten years ago:

> What is important about St Paul ... is his consistent method of yoking ... [theology and ethics] together and recognising – and making plain also to his readers – that the one is influenced powerfully by the other. A perfect example of this method is to be found in the first two chapters of his Epistle to the Phillippians, the centre-piece of which is the so-called Song of Christ's Glory. In these two chapters St Paul is exhorting his readers to a particular way of life, and doing so firmly within the highly theological context of the life, death and resurrection of Jesus Christ himself, and the indwelling of the Holy Spirit. The church at Philippi is to live in a certain way precisely because it believes certain things. For St Paul, theology and Christian practice are merely two sides of the same coin, two expressions of the one reality: our faith in God and our life for God.[6]

Biblical theology, even in the hands of its most subtle and sustained exponent, St Paul, remains firmly in its place as a useful tool for Christian living, rather than an exercise in quasi-philosophical speculation.

Such did not remain the case during the succeeding few centuries which were to prove so formative for the whole of the subsequent history of theology. The active, willing God of the Bible became increasingly imprisoned within the categories of metaphysics, and theology became ever more concerned with God's being and with intellectual puzzles such as how divine and human natures might be satisfactorily reconciled in the incarnation. God increasingly became an object of philosophical speculation, and one sometimes wonders whether the 'God of Abraham, Isaac and Jacob' (and of Jesus too, of course) would be able to recognise himself in the formulations of the various Ecumenical Councils!

This turn towards an interest in the metaphysics of being – which has remained central to theology ever since – leads us to the third area in which theology is in permanent danger of being taken prisoner by philosophy. This danger arises as a result of the potent fusion of theology's own obsession with a metaphysics of being with the Enlightenment's conviction of the supremacy of human reason. The offspring of this union has been the reign of ontology, which has proved to be something of a cuckoo in the theological nest, in that it has succeeded in jettisoning other forms of reasoning. Furthermore, it has also itself spawned the strange hybrid, 'onto-theology' which, if followed, represents successful theological suicide, at least as far as having any meaningful connection with the living God of scripture is concerned. If this is to be avoided, theology needs to remain in touch with human experience and praxis and with the God of scripture and revelation, and to be constantly aware that human language and reason can never adequately understand or represent (let alone pin down in metaphysical categories) the ultimate majesty and mystery of God.

In an excellent, although necessarily brief, overview of a paper by Merold Westphal, John D. Caputo and Michael J. Scanlon deftly outline how the dangerous slide into onto-theology occurs, point out how and why it represents a betrayal of the theological task proper, and indicate how the slide may be halted:

> In 'Overcoming Onto-theology,' Merold Westphal argues that theology does not become onto-theology simply by employing philosophical concepts like omniscience or foreknowledge to elucidate the biblical understanding of God or even by speaking of God as the Highest Being. Theology only becomes onto-theology when philosophers or theologians sell their soul to philosophy's project of rendering the whole of reality intelligible to human understanding by using God to do so. Thus, onto-theology consists of the pride that refuses to accept the limits of human knowledge. The critique of onto-theology is directed not at what we say

about God but at how we say it, to what purpose, in the service of what project. Much of Westphal's paper is a conversation with Heidegger on God, theology, and the atheistic character of philosophy. His project is to appropriate Heidegger's critique of onto-theology for theistic theology, which is authentic to the extent that it is in service to the praxis of the believer.[7]

For the sake of its own self-preservation, theology must distinguish itself clearly from ontology. Indeed – and in my view rightly – Phillip Blond goes even further and argues that theology must be not merely separate from, but also superior to, ontology:

> The relationship ... that pertains for theology with respect to ontology must be one of absolute superiority. By this I mean that theology is the discourse about the origin of being. For this reason ontology cannot account for theology; ontology can offer no discourse as to its own origin. Being will always, as Heidegger himself noted, find itself already there, already distributed in beings. Being is not accessible except through beings. Just as Hegel was never actually able to buy fruit itself; that is, he was unable to purchase a fruit that was not also an apple or a pear, so ontology will never be able to grasp Being apart from beings. Ontology, as Aristotle himself acknowledged, can never grasp or account for Being in its most general (and most specific) form; such a horizon is quite simply beyond its scope. For it is here that ontology, unable to give an account of the ground of its own system of classification, betrays itself, as it must, to a theological account of its origin.[8]

No more than it should be enslaved by the legacy of the patristic era or the Enlightenment should theology be in thrall to ontology.

The exorcising of these various demons, which had largely taken possession of theology's soul, has substantial and life-enhancing consequences for theology. Put succinctly, theology becomes once again its own master. It has its own subject matter and its own rationale, and it is allowed to experiment with new concepts and new categories of thought. Admittedly not all of these will prove helpful or enduring. Some will be inadequate, some may prove to be theological dead-ends, some may even turn out to be unhelpful or misleading. But, refreshingly, theology is not necessarily and irrevocably locked into one particular thought world and set of metaphysical concepts, and nor is it governed by whatever the prevailing philosophical viewpoint of the time may happen to be. It is free to attempt to bear witness to the nature and activity of the living God of scripture and revelation and thereby to inform the lives, witness and prayers of believers; and if this means finding fresher and more compelling forms of expression to replace some of the rather worn and weary (and irrelevant to most people's worldview) metaphysical constructs of past doctrinal formulations, then so much the better. Having sprung the bars of theology's prison, it is my intention to do precisely this, in that most central doctrine of all – christology.

Notes

1. Tertullian, *De praescriptione haereticorum*, Chapter Seven.
2. John D. Caputo and Michael J. Scanlon (eds), *God, the Gift, and Postmodernism*, Bloomington and Indianapolis, Indiana University Press, 1999, p 10.
3. Phillip Blond, (ed), *Post-Secular Philosophy: Between Philosophy and Theology*, London and New York, Routledge, 1998, p 30.
4. Dorothy L. Sayers, *The Mind of the Maker*, London, Methuen, 1941, p 146.
5. Caputo & Scanlon, p 2.
6. Stephen R. White, *A Space for Belief: The Place of Theology in Faith*, Dublin, Columba Press, 2006, p 73.
7. Caputo & Scanlon, p 13.
8. Blond, p 12.

CHAPTER FOUR

Becoming the Christ

The removal of the shade of Augustinianism and of the stranglehold on theology exercised by classical metaphysics and Enlightenment philosophy opens up an entirely new answer to a crucial christological question: where should christology begin? The answer to this question will clearly dictate the greater part of one's christological conclusions, and for any theologian there is – or at least has been, particularly under the baneful influence of St Augustine – a tremendous temptation to begin with the 'finished product': that is, with Jesus Christ crucified, risen and ascended, and then (simply?) to ask the metaphysical question: 'How can this be?'

This is an attractive and entirely understandable route to take for at least two reasons. First, it sets a neat and tidy speculative, metaphysical problem which is, in principle, capable of being answered, and the answering of such problems is itself – rather like the proving of an abstruse mathematical theorem – a deeply satisfying intellectual exercise. Secondly, it also begins from what feels like a reassuringly safe place, both doctrinally and devotionally: the divinity of Jesus has already been safely acknowledged as a starting point, and all that follows is then done from within the safety of a good orthodox framework. The theologian is, as it were, working from within the familiar territory of home.

To step outside this world is painful, even threatening, and yet I believe that it is also essential if we are to re-envision christology and breathe new life into it. The need for a different approach when dealing with Jesus (and, indeed, with the gospels in general) is astutely put by Philip Yancy:

> Pulitzer prize-winning historian Barbara Tuchmann insists on one rule in writing history: no 'flash-forwards'. When she

was writing about the Battle of the Bulge in World War II, for example, she resisted the temptation to include 'Of course we all know how this turned out' asides. In point of fact, the Allied troops involved in the Battle of the Bulge did not know how the battle would turn out. From the look of things, they could well be driven right back to the beaches of Normandy where they had come from. A historian who wants to retain any semblance of tension and drama in events as they unfold dare not flash-forward to another, all seeing point of view. Do so, and all tension melts away. Rather, a good historian re-creates for the reader the conditions of the history being described, conveying a sense that 'you were there'.

That, I concluded, is the problem with most of our writing and thinking about Jesus. We read the gospels through the flash-forward lenses of church councils, like Nicea and Chalcedon, through the church's studied attempts to make sense of him.[1]

To refuse to 'flash-forward' in the context of christology means, I think, to do two things, both of which will be attempted in this chapter. It means, first, to leave the 'finished product' of Jesus Christ to one side for the time being and to focus solely on the person of Jesus of Nazareth; and secondly, to re-read and re-interpret the gospel records with the concept of 'becoming' in mind, even though this may appear to be an alien concept to the gospels themselves. In fact, as we shall see, there is an implicit awareness of becoming present in these accounts, even though their explicit message is that of the proclamation of Jesus as the Christ.

At first sight, then, such a re-reading of the gospels may look like a lost cause: after all, the earliest of them begins with the un-ambiguous announcement: 'The beginning of the gospel of Jesus Christ the Son of God.' No room for much re-interpretation here, one might think! But the gospels are not as single-layered or monochrome as this opening statement of St Mark's gospel might have us imagine, and running through all of them one can trace a half-buried thread of becoming on Jesus' part, moments when his destiny or identity or both are being forged by conscious choice; and it is these moments and their profound significance which we shall attempt to trace here.

At this point, however, and before we proceed any further with this task, two things must be noted, one in relation to the intentions of the gospel writers themselves, and the other in relation to the historical reliability – or lack of it – of any or all of these gospel records.

First, then, the intentions of the four gospel writers. These are, generally speaking, overt and straightforward, and my purpose is not to argue that black is white and that the intentions of the evangelists were anything other than what they claim to be: that is, to inform, to proclaim, and to inspire belief in the reader or the hearer – belief in Jesus precisely as the Christ, crucified, risen and ascended. Thus, for example, Luke says that he has written his gospel, 'so that you may know the truth concerning the things about which you have been instructed', (1:4, *NRSV*) and John writes his account 'so that you may come to believe that Jesus is the Messiah, the Son of God, and that through believing you may have life in his name' (20:31, *NRSV*). So forthright and uncompromising are the evangelists in their conviction as to their task and in their presentation of their message that it would be sheer folly to attempt to suggest that anything else at all was their overt intention.

However, modern (or rather post-modern) literary theory has offered us some new ways of approaching texts, and whatever the possible excesses of such movements as post-structuralism and deconstructionism, we have at least been taught to look behind the express intention of a text and to read alongside this a number of other motifs or themes which may be sub-conscious or even entirely unconscious on the part of the writer, but which may yet have a substantial impact upon the reader. Such is the status of the theme of becoming in the gospels. Yes, certainly the evangelists themselves were writing from the perspective of seeing Jesus as the Christ, and wishing to present him from the first as being such, but moving barely beneath the surface of their texts there runs, like a strong undercurrent, a remembrance of decisive moments in the career of Jesus which are open to a very different interpretation from that which the evangelists – and following them the bulk of subsequent Christian history – have placed upon them. The purpose of this chapter, therefore, is not to subvert the gospel texts entirely, or to attempt to offer a new explanation of their intention, but rather to re-arrange some of the elements of the story of Jesus such that a hidden motif may become more explicit and may point not so much to the *a priori* divine Christ of the gospels, but rather to the person of Jesus of Nazareth who stands in shadowy fashion behind the church's official portraits of him.

This invocation of the historical figure of Jesus leads us naturally on to the second of the issues which I have suggested must be briefly commented upon here: the historical reliability of the gospel records. Plainly there is much at stake here, and it is, furthermore, notoriously hard to prove that any particular episode in the gospels actually happened, or even that there is a core of historical truth behind the traditions, successive redactions and final 'authorship' of the gospels.

Impossible it may be to prove, therefore, but it is at least likely that such a core of truth exists behind the three episodes on which I intend to concentrate, simply because in themselves (although they have, of course, been re-worked within the gospels to make precisely the opposite point) they represent a potentially uncomfortable alternative to the predominantly divinising perspective from within which the gospels essentially operate. They have, I suggest, been included in the narratives not because they naturally fitted with what the evangelists were trying to do – far from it, and hence the need for extensive re-working in order to make them fit – but rather because there is historical truth about the figure of Jesus contained within them. The episodes in question, then, come respectively from the beginning, the middle and the end of Jesus' ministry, and to the first of these, the temptation narratives – which we have already encountered in another context in Chapter Two – we must now turn.

In a sense it is not to the exact content of the narratives, but rather to the mere fact of their existence at all that I wish to draw attention, for they are potentially entirely subversive of any form of christology 'from above', or of any attempt to present a necessarily divine Jesus. This fact is, of course, not alluded to at all in the heavily stylised and mythological accounts of Jesus' temptation in the three synoptic gospels. What we are actually presented with in these accounts is a patently divine figure quite literally 'seeing off' the tempter, having serenely overcome him in a battle of scriptural quotations. What is potentially so subversive is not these accounts themselves, but their explicit admission that Jesus was in fact – although undoubtedly not in the precise and limited forms both in number and duration presented in these accounts – tempted. And this, if it is addressed squarely, rather than viewed through the gospels' re-working of it, is a staggering admission. So staggering in fact that nowhere does any of the gospels dare to consider its real implications, and nowhere likewise do any of the gospels bring us to believe in the reality of that temptation – for who can really believe in the stylised and formal three temptations presented by the gospels?

At least, however, these stories admit that Jesus was tempted, and this allows us room to move outside the narrow confines of the gospel accounts themselves and look at the reality of that temptation. The principal reality is that if Jesus was tempted, then, by definition – and contrary to the appearances of the biblical presentation of this experience – he could have succumbed to temptation. He could, at any point in his career, knowingly and wilfully have sinned. He could have sinned in any of the countless ways in which human beings have sinned before and since. We may well wish to hold that he did not in fact sin, but this must never blind us to the simple fact that he could have done.

A secondary reality to be taken into account (as we have briefly argued earlier) is that if we admit that Jesus was tempted, then we also have to admit that such temptation would not have been of such limited duration and scope as in the temptation narratives, but would rather have been – in common with the experience of the rest of humanity – a lifelong condition embracing many different forms of temptation. It is this fact which – contrary to popular and indeed also ecclesial and even episcopal outcry – makes even such a production as Martin Scorcese's film *The Last Temptation of Christ* not blasphemous, but simply true to the possibilities inherent in a truly and fully human Jesus. If he could be tempted, then why not in this way as in any other; and, of course, the film proclaims that tempted though he (fictionally in this case) was, this temptation, like all others, was resisted, and the brutality of the cross sinlessly endured. What, indeed, could be more orthodox?

Orthodox, yes, but even by itself entirely destructive of any philosophically necessary connection between the person of Jesus and the figure of the Christ. For such a unity to be necessary, the almost shocking possibilities to which we have alluded could not possibly have been the case, for Jesus would need to have been 'pre-programmed' so as to be unable to sin in order that the divine purpose should not even be exposed to the possibility of being thwarted; and then we have already fallen into the trap of downplaying Jesus' humanity and opened ourselves to Gregory of Nazianzus' picture of a partial redeemer only, since, 'that which he has not assumed [in this case the potential for human frailty] he has not healed,'[2] and thereby also making a mockery of our redemption, for it is precisely this frailty of human nature which produces the need for that redemption in the first place. And furthermore if this is the case, then the temptation narratives themselves are logically redundant, since for a pre-programmed being such as this there can be no temptation, this being a contentless and therefore meaningless concept. Necessity is destructive of full humanity, and the logical, if to some unpalatable, consequence of this is that already, taking only the reality of temptation into account, the human being Jesus of Nazareth did not – at any stage in his career – have to be the Christ. Quite simply and bluntly, he might equally well not have been the Christ. He might, indeed, simply have failed to become the Christ.

The second episode to which I wish to draw attention is that in which Jesus questions his disciples with the words, 'Who do people say I am?' and then more urgently, 'But what about you? Who do you say I am?' (Mark 8:27-29 and parallels.) Here again, as with the temptation of Jesus, the gospel narrative is carefully shaped to provide the right answer, such that the question becomes almost a rhetorical one serving to establish the divine identity of the gospel's central character. Furthermore, it is not only carefully shaped but also equally carefully placed (especially by Mark) to illustrate with almost brutal yet deft irony an extended exploration of the polarities of sight and blindness, both physical and, more significantly, spiritual.

Aside, though, from this thoroughly literary and didactic use of the episode, we may reasonably assume that the question (or, more accurately, the linked pair of questions) goes back in essence to Jesus himself, and we may legitimately wonder about the precise content and especially about the tone of voice in which they were spoken, and about the reasoning behind the asking of such questions. For it would surely be unlikely that Jesus would have asked such questions primarily to elicit – as seems to be the case in the gospel account – a neatly staged confession of faith from his hearers. If these questions do – as indeed I think they do – go back to Jesus himself, then one might well imagine them being asked in a much more open-ended and hesitant fashion than the evangelists allow for. They are the questions not of a Jesus seeking a confession of faith in himself, but of a Jesus beginning to come to terms with a sense of divine vocation and possibility, and perhaps also with the dawnings of a sense of becoming towards sonship, and seeking through his followers to clarify that vocation, and with it indeed his own identity and sense of becoming. Hence, I suggest, the unusual urgency in the tone of the second question which comes through even in the different repackagings of the story in the various gospels. This urgency of tone is deftly highlighted by Oliver Davies, although admittedly in the service of a very different argument from the one advanced here:

> Jesus seems dissatisfied with these answers and asks them directly, 'But who do you say that I am?' where the emphatic form of 'you' used here ... sets up an opposition between 'the people' ... and Jesus' disciples, who are themselves to be set apart by their response to his question.[3]

If the purpose of Jesus' question in the evangelists' presentation is to draw out a confession of faith (in a persona and sonship in which Jesus is already assured and 'at home'), then almost any form of the second question would have sufficed: a casual, 'And you?' would, for example, provide exactly the same opportunity for confession.

The actual tone of the question, however, is entirely at odds with this overt intention. It is as if, having asked, 'Who do people say I am?', Jesus has received from his disciples a range of answers, none of which resonates with his own still emerging sense of identity and purpose, and so the question is turned onto the disciples themselves and asked with redoubled force, and almost with a sense of desperation, of needing to receive an answer which will help to make sense of Jesus' own experience, and asked without any certainty at all as to exactly what answer will be given: 'But what about you? Who do you say I am?' Then, at least, comes back the answer which must have at once reassured and shattered Jesus in almost equal measure: 'You are the Christ.'

Coming as it does from a primarily literary rather than theological perspective, it is instructive to see the novelist Norman Mailer also interpreting this exchange as being formative of Jesus' identity as the Christ. He writes:

> There were nights when I would awaken and not know who I was. Once, passing through the town of Caesarea Philippi, I asked my disciples: 'Who do they say I am?'
>
> And some answered that I was said to be John the Baptist. Others spoke of Elijah. Still others told me: 'They do not know, but think you are one of the old prophets.'
>
> And I said, and my heart was pounding: 'But who do you say I am?'
>
> And Peter – it may be that he was thinking of how I had walked upon the water – asked gently: 'Can one say that you are the Christ?'
>
> Since I felt like an ordinary man in all ways but one, I could love Peter for the strength that his conviction gave me. Now I knew with more certainty than before that I must be the Son of God. Yet how could I be certain of that if no man recognised me?[4]

If, as I have argued, Jesus' identity was in process of becoming, then it is hardly surprising that he should frequently have told his disciples not to speak openly of that identity (as is the case immediately following Peter's confession in St Marks's gospel), and indeed Jesus himself does not do so until after the last of the three episodes of becoming upon which we focus here, the Garden of Gethsemane, by which time the harsh road of becoming had been travelled almost to its bitter but glorious end. If, in temptation, we see a Jesus who might not have become the Christ, then here in his questioning of the disciples we see a Jesus who is himself discovering and coming to terms with precisely the possibility of becoming the Christ.

Finally, then, in the Garden of Gethsemane, we receive a glimpse of a Jesus who through and beyond suffering freely chooses that road and that possibility of becoming the Christ – whether we envisage him as being consciously aware of that possibility or not. Once again the exact historical accuracy of the scene is not of the first importance, but we can well imagine that Jesus (like anyone else in such a situation) would have prayed for deliverance from the fate which would by now have seemed (as indeed it turned out to be) well-nigh imminent. But that deliverance was not forthcoming, and as Jesus goes to meet his accusers he chooses (not for the first time, but certainly for the most momentous time) to continue to walk along the road of becoming which had begun so many years previously. At this point especially, Christianity suffers from the 'flash-forward' syndrome forbidden by Barbara Tuchmann. We know what actually happened – the arrest, trial, crucifixion and resurrection – but we need forcefully to be reminded that even at this late stage it did not have to be this way. Such a forceful reminder is, perhaps surprisingly, offered by Catherine Marshall – surprising both in that it was first written approaching fifty years ago, and also in that she is otherwise of a generally theologically conservative and evangelical school of thought. Compellingly she says:

> For let us not mistake it. Christ could have avoided that cross. He did not have to go to Jerusalem that last time. He could have compromised with the priests, bargained with Caiaphas. The disciples were probably right in thinking that he could have capitalised on his following, appeased Judas, and set up the beginning of an earthly empire. Later Pilate would all but beg him to say the right words so that he might release him. Even in the Garden of Gethsemane on the night of betrayal, Christ had plenty of time and opportunity to flee.[5]

At any time up to and including his arrest Jesus could simply have walked away, ended his ministry, returned quietly to

Galilee and kept well out of the limelight and out of trouble. Indeed, even after his arrest it is quite possible (although not entirely certain) that he might well have been able to talk his way out of trouble had he chosen to do so. A simple denial of all personal significance and a promise of good behaviour in the future might well have done the trick – and then what of the Christ? And this possibility of choosing not to continue has again to be taken utterly seriously if Jesus is to be viewed as a fully human being and not as an automaton in the hands of divinity. In Gethsemane we are confronted by a Jesus who could have chosen not to become the Christ.

In these three episodes, then, and doubtless in others also if one wished to trawl further through the pages of the gospels, a yawning chasm has opened up between the human figure of the man Jesus and any sense of pre-ordained metaphysical and philosophical necessity as far as any unity between him and the Christ is concerned. We may still wish to claim unity between them, but that unity must be acknowledged to be entirely contingent upon the continuous choosing of becoming and on the continual realisation of potential. Through this, we may well wish to claim, Jesus became (and therefore remains for all eternity) the Christ, but that becoming was a life-long process which did not have to happen at all and in which the divine will could have been thwarted at any, and indeed, every moment.

Notes
1. Philip Yancey, *The Jesus I Never Knew*, London, Marshall Pickering, 1995, p 22.
2. Gregory of Nazianzus, *Letter 101*.
3. Oliver Davies, *A Theology of Compassion*, London, SCM Press, 2001, p 214.
4. Norman Mailer, *The Gospel According to the Son*, New York and London, Random House and Little, Brown and Company, 1997.
5. Catherine Marshall, *Beyond Ourselves*, London, Sydney and Auckland, Hodder and Stoughton, 1969, p 103. (First Pub. Peter Davies Ltd, 1962.)

CHAPTER FIVE

The Divine Weakness

In the course of the previous chapter we asserted that christology must begin from a radically different starting point from
that of traditional metaphysics, ontology or philosophy: namely,
with the categories of becoming and realised potential. The principal reason for claiming this is the conviction that full justice
must be done to the humanity of Jesus and that this humanity
must at no point be 'swamped', as throughout Christian history
it so often has been, by divinity, a conviction powerfully expressed by Albert Nolan who insisted that 'Jesus is a much un-
derrated man ... To deprive this man of his humanity is to deprive him of his greatness.'[1] At the same time, however, it is vital
that whilst christology must be true to our understanding of
humanity, it must also (and equally) be true to our understanding of God. It is therefore essential that the correlation between
what we know or infer of God and the model of incarnational becoming which we have posited be investigated a little more thoroughly before we can presume to proceed any further.

Our 'knowledge' of God is rooted in a variety of aspects of
our life, both intellectual and emotional. Theologically speaking
it is located primarily in the given data of Christian and Jewish
history: that is, in revelation and, however one wishes to describe them, in the classical Anglican triad of scripture, tradition
and reason. At another level, however, this broadly intellectual
and communal knowledge of God is complemented by our own
personal (and also again communal) experience of God: our
theologising is 'cashed out' in our experience of God in prayer
and worship and in all the minutiae of daily living. Clearly we
shall need to examine some of the more overtly theological aspects of our understanding of God in due course, but it is with
the immediacy of lived Christian experience of God that I wish
to begin, for the simple reason that however important our

theologising may be – and I believe that it is indeed absolutely essential – nonetheless it is this lived experience which forms, devotionally and ethically, the 'cutting edge' of our faith.

So how do we experience God? What seems to be the characteristic mode of his activity, and what seems to be the nature of his relationship with the created order, ourselves included? Perhaps the first thing to be said is that our perception of God and his nature and activity has altered quite dramatically over the last few centuries, and it would not, I think, have been possible to frame a concept such as the becoming described in the previous chapter, in any earlier age. Thus if one looks back to almost any of the more 'primitive' religions, and even to the vast bulk of Jewish and Christian history (and certainly to that history as it is recorded in the scriptures) we appear to be dealing with a predominantly – and often very heavy-handedly – interventionist God. To him directly are ascribed dramatic events of nature, the rise and fall of kings, the fortunes of individuals and of nations, and the health of both mind and body. His pleasure and wrath are overtly expressed and issue in specific consequences of blessing or curse, weal or woe, for the individuals and nations involved.

In more recent years, though, whether one wishes to date the beginning of change to the Reformation or to the Renaissance, or to the Enlightenment, or to Victorian scepticism, or even to twentieth-century modernism or post-modernism, all of this has changed for ever. As we have come to know increasingly more about the workings of the universe, of our own planet and of our own minds and bodies, there has arisen a corresponding sense that the natural world just is the natural world, and that there is no need to invoke God's direct intervention to explain all of its endless diversity, beauty and terror. Furthermore, this new-found freedom of creation from perpetual divine intervention has resulted in a parallel freedom for humanity within it. For we do not now see God as directly controlling the destiny of kings or visiting death or disease on people as punishment and so on. If the natural world is allowed to go its own way, so too human beings have discovered that they too may follow their own path – and it is a path which God will not prevent them from taking. This is not to say that God (or his authority) have been banished, but merely to say that our perception of these things has undergone a sea-change, a dramatic paradigm shift. Our own experience – and certainly that of the whole Christian community – is that God may indeed influence us through our praying and through our moral senses, but that nonetheless our freedom is genuinely our own and we can seek or thwart God's will, and in neither case will we be overridden by divine fiat. No longer do we perceive God as intervening to overthrow or override human decisions and choices: they are our own, and for better or for worse we (and, almost incredible as it may seem, God) will have to live with them.

From a contemporary perspective, then, human freedom and a divine respect for and acceptance of that freedom appear to be some of the key elements in the relationship between creator and creatures. If this is true of the entire human race then it seems at once illogical and absurd to deny to one particular human being the exercise of that freedom. If it is true that our life is one of constant choice, of becoming, and of the realisation of potential, then it would seem that for incarnation to be incarnation in any fully meaningful fashion, it must also be true for the earthly life of Jesus himself, and not as a regrettable aspect to be glossed over if at all possible, but as an element as central for Jesus and his life as it is in our own lives.

If this freedom to become is fundamental to incarnation when viewed from a human perspective, then I would also suggest that it is no less so from a divine perspective, for, as hinted previously, our freedom has consequences for God. These derive from the fact that through the granting of this freedom, and equally through his continued respect for it such that he will not overthrow it or limit our exercise of it to 'unimportant' areas of life, God has effectively put the performance of his will on earth quite literally into our hands. His will is ours to do or to frustrate, and this is so both within the individual human life and in the wider sphere of the totality of life on our planet, as eco-theology is somewhat belatedly endeavouring to make plain. As Christians we naturally perceive the incarnation as a pivotal point in the exercise (and fulfilment) of God's will, but is it not likely that even (and perhaps especially) at such a crucial moment, he should once again have placed the realisation of that will into human hands, in this case those of Jesus of Nazareth?

Becoming incarnate through human choosing as well as divine will would appear to be as essential if God is to remain true to himself as it is if humanity is to be true to itself.

So far we have been arguing solely from the nature of God as we perceive him, and how that nature might be most fully and properly expressed in incarnation. It is equally possible (and equally important) though, that we are able to reach much the same conclusions on strictly theological grounds drawn from scripture and from the traditions of the Christian church. The conclusions may perhaps be unfamiliar within those scriptures and that tradition, but the materials from which they are reached are there nonetheless.

One of the most basic building-blocks of Christian theology, then, is the notion of God as creator, reflected in mythological form in the creation narratives of the book of Genesis. It may be many years since either of these narratives has been seen (except perhaps by some extreme fundamentalists) as anything other than a pictorial, symbolic and imaginative account of creation, but Christian theology continues to find within them theological, even if not exact historical, truth. Such is the case with our most basic understanding of what it means to be a human being. It is true that we no longer see ourselves as being descended from a historical pair of proto-parents named Adam and Eve, but the story still commands our respect and attention in its proclamation of our creature/creator relationship with God, its exploration of our relationship with the rest of creation, and its profound and yet necessarily puzzling suggestion that we are made in the 'image and likeness' of God himself.

The precise meaning of this phrase, the 'image and likeness' of God, has been tirelessly explored by countless theologians from Irenaeus onwards, as has the vexed question of whether there is any significant difference in meaning or connotation between the two Hebrew words which are translated as 'image' and 'likeness' respectively. However, the precise epistemological niceties of the phrase are not at issue here. What is important about the phrase in this context is that it implies that there is some essential continuity – or perhaps even consanguinity – of being between ourselves and God. Plainly there are vast differences: we lack any of the divine attributes of omniscience, omnipotence, absolute goodness and so on, but nonetheless there is a meaningful ontological connection (even if we cannot articulate in what, precisely, it consists) between ourselves and God, and this understanding of ourselves has (or should have) far-reaching consequences for our understanding of incarnation.

From a very early period, then, perhaps as early as the mid-second century, virtually all discussion of incarnation has been conducted in the rarefied language and thought-world of Greek and Latin metaphysics, and this has proved (as we saw in some detail in Chapter Three) at once a blessing and a curse for the history of Christian theology. On the positive side, it has enabled some of the most brilliant thinkers of successive ages to develop complex and yet clear-cut formulae for belief and understanding of nature both human and divine, and it has fostered the production of neat creedal statements and allowed for lines of demarcation to be drawn between orthodoxy and heresy.

More negatively, however, it has, especially through this last function of defining orthodoxy, almost by definition effectively stifled any attempts to develop an alternative approach to incarnation or to begin the discussion from a different starting-place. Even more importantly than this, perhaps, an exclusively metaphysical approach also suffers from an intrinsic weakness to which, in an earlier chapter, we have already alluded. This is its insistence on employing 'human' and 'divine' as two quite distinct and fixed ontological states, and leads to a feeling that however cleverly and technically proficiently the metaphysics is employed, nonetheless what is being attempted is an effort to pour oil and water into the same container and mix them. Incarnation on this model is almost doomed to end up looking like some kind of divine conjuring trick, and the oil and water of divinity and humanity produce merely a somewhat unattractive emulsion, the constituent parts of which are always threatening to separate out once again.

In complete contrast to this, if one begins from the idea of there being some definite innate connection between, and even similarity of being between the human and the divine – such that it can properly be said that we are made in the 'image' and 'likeness' of God – then the possibility of incarnation immediately begins to make more sense. Incarnation is not something which is foisted upon an intrinsically alien human nature 'from above', but rather it is a logical consequence of the possibilities inherent in our own human nature. If, in every instance, human nature reflects something of God's nature, then it is quite possible – although no less amazing for that – that in one instance, human nature, through constant choosing and becoming and realising its full potential, should reflect the totality of God's nature insofar as this can be expressed within the limitations of a human mind and body.

Similarly, just as it reflects our theological understanding of our own human nature, so too this model of incarnation based on becoming also reflects our theological understanding of the entire creation and of God's activity as its creator. Again, our perceptions have changed rapidly and radically over the last one hundred and fifty years or so, but the time is now long past when the world – and indeed the universe – was seen as a fixed, static entity ordered in its entirety from the very beginning by God. Now, indeed, we do actually see the universe, and within it our world, as being a place of perpetual becoming. Different species rise and fall. Stars are born and die. Environments change (even without our own, and usually destructive, help), and even the earth itself is still constantly in formation as volcanoes erupt and decline, coastlines advance and recede, water levels rise or fall and so on. There is endless flux and constant becoming, and our faith adds that this has a *telos*, a purpose, and that in a new creation of a new heaven and a new earth (however that is to be understood and whatever it might turn out to look like), all of this potential and becoming will at last be fully realised. Becoming, rather than stasis of any sort, would appear to be the hallmark of God's activity, within the finite realms of matter and history at least.

Becoming appears, therefore, to be a viable theological tool with which to approach the incarnation. It also has one further claim to merit attention, which is that it solves – or rather does away with – one of the most perennially problematic aspects of incarnation as traditionally understood. That is the issue of *kenosis*, the question of how unlimited divinity can dwell without essential diminution in limited humanity. This has always presented a problem for any ontologically fixed and metaphysical approach to incarnation, and indeed, always will do, for within the terms of this particular debate there just is no entirely satisfactory way around it. Put at its simplest, the problem is this: God is defined as impassible and incapable of change or loss, and yet in becoming human there is, by definition, change and loss involved. The solution to this has been to invoke the idea of a divine outpouring or self-emptying (often based on Philippians 2:4-11) in which aspects of divinity (such as omniscience) are voluntarily renounced in the incarnation. They are therefore not lost or changed, merely foregone or laid aside for the duration, and God's unchangeable nature is thereby safeguarded. No form of this 'solution', whether strong or weak, has, however, been entirely convincing, and all of them smack strongly of theological special pleading. God may not be able to do that which is logically impossible or self-contradictory, such as creating a square circle, but where he has failed, theologians seem to have succeeded admirably!

Yet again the problem essentially stems from the limitations of metaphysics and from an insistence on a fixed ontological divide between the human and the divine which can only be bridged – and this remains true even if one attempts to construct a christology 'from below' in the traditional framework – from the divine side with divinity in some sense 'assuming' humanity.

By contrast, the model which we have been developing here allows for, and indeed demands, an entirely different understanding of the relationship between human and divine in the incarnation. According to traditional metaphysics – in which incarnation simply 'happened' as soon as the infant Jesus was born, or perhaps even conceived – there must always be some degree of divine emptying out, even if not necessarily a full-blown *kenosis* in order for incarnation to be accomplished. If instead, however, we employ the category of becoming as a tool for understanding the incarnation, then what is conceived of as taking place is not God emptying himself out in order to become human, but God progressively (through every moment of choice and decision such as we considered in Chapter Four) filling and indwelling humanity in order to draw it ultimately towards and indeed into divinity. No longer is there any sense of divine emptying or self-limitation. Jesus is limited in his humanity, certainly, but this humanity is journeying, through a life-long process of choosing, of becoming, and of the realisation of its full potential, towards divinity.

At this point, one further potential objection (quite separate from the previously noted problems with metaphysics, philosophy and St Augustine) must be noted, and this is simply that if Jesus could achieve this full realisation of potential and union with God, then why, in principle, should another – or even many others – not do so also; and what does this possibility infer about the uniqueness of Jesus and the Trinitarian nature of God? This objection will be discussed in Chapter Seven, after we have considered another possible stumbling-block, the concept of the pre-existence of the Christ in Chapter Six. In the course of these two chapters I hope to continue to demonstrate that the approach to christology advocated here is neither illogical in itself, nor incompatible with much of the Christian tradition; following which, in the remainder of this study, I shall attempt to elucidate some of the wider theological and ethical implications of this model of incarnation and Christ-ship. For the present, though, we must re-inhabit, at least briefly, the realm of metaphysics, and turn from the becoming in time of Jesus to the timeless pre-existence of the Christ.

Notes:
1. Albert Nolan, *Jesus Before Christianity*, Maryknoll NY, Orbis Books, 1978, p 117.

CHAPTER SIX

Jesus and the Riddle of Trinitarian Pre-existence

We have established already that although the arguments put forward here may differ substantially from those advanced by a more traditional ontologically and metaphysically based approach to Christology, nonetheless they are by no means entirely at odds with either scripture or several other well-established areas of theological discussion. It is only to be expected, however, that there may well appear to be points of conflict, or even points at which any alternative approach is simply ruled out of court by the weight of tradition. It is my intention in this chapter and in the succeeding one to illustrate that in the case of at least two of these areas the conflict is one in appearance only, and does not in fact betoken any deep-seated clash of theological method or even – though it does involve a substantial change of emphasis – of doctrinal conclusion.

At the heart of our Christian faith, then, is the concept (and, of course, the experience) of God as Trinity: Father, Son and Holy Spirit, all co-existing from all eternity, without beginning and without end. It might, of course, be argued that this is only a pictorial, symbolic representation of God, produced by finite human minds, and that therefore it bears no substantial relationship to the reality of God as he is 'in himself' – whatever this might turn out to be. This would represent a rather substantial ducking of the issue, however, and one must, I feel, be prepared to engage with, rather than summarily dismiss, such a central aspect of our faith. It would appear to have been the settled conviction of orthodox Christians for two thousand years that God is Trinitarian in his essence and that the Christ/Son did enjoy pre-existence, and the question must therefore squarely be faced of how this may be said to be compatible with a theology of incarnation which is progressive rather than instantaneous and absolute, and which begins from the very 'un-timeless' concept of becoming.

Probably the most obviously significant scriptural passage in connection with pre-existence, in that it has formed the backdrop to so much of christological thinking from the days of Justin Martyr onwards, is the so-called 'Prologue' to St John's gospel, a passage which, because of its importance, it is worth quoting fairly substantially:

> In the beginning was the Word, and the Word was with God, and the Word was God. He was in the beginning with God; all things were made through him, and without him was not anything made that was made ... And the Word became flesh and dwelt among us, full of grace and truth; we have beheld his glory, glory as of the only Son from the Father. (John 1:1-3, 14)

It is essential in considering this passage to be absolutely clear about what St John is saying, and equally clear about what he is not in fact saying. It is all too often assumed – even sometimes, as we shall see, by the theologically extremely well-educated – that John is declaring the pre-existence of Jesus Christ, lock, stock and barrel: that, however one wishes to imagine such a thing, the Second Person of the Trinity, identified precisely as Jesus Christ, existed in and with God from before all time and was ready at the right moment to descend from heaven in human form. This common interpretative error, especially as it appears to non-theologians, is perfectly illustrated by Rachel Feldhay Brenner in her study of women writers and the holocaust, and the confusion between the Christ and the person of Jesus of Nazareth is highlighted brilliantly, if also inadvertently. She writes:

> The idea of a Christ who coexisted with God since the creation of the world is not new ... The hymn [John 1:1-14] presents Jesus as the pre-existent Redeemer.[1]

This identification may or may not reflect what John intended to say, but vitally importantly it does not reflect what John actually does say.

For nowhere does John actually say that Jesus the man is the pre-existent Word or Son. There appears to be in John's thought, and certainly there is in his language, a crucial distance between the two ideas of the pre-existence of the Word and the physical 'bearer' of that Word, the man, Jesus of Nazareth. What John proclaims is not a Jesus who is in any sense pre-existent, but rather a pre-existent Word which, at a specific moment in time, 'became flesh and dwelt among us' in the person of Jesus, and this is a radically – and crucially importantly – different concept from positing the pre-existence of Jesus Christ *in toto*.

But it is not only non-theologians who are prone to confuse the personae of Jesus of Nazareth and the Christ, and it is also not only in the context of St John's Prologue that such confusion occurs. Even in an otherwise excellent book, specifically on New Testament christology, Frank J. Matera, in a discussion of St Paul's Epistle to the Galatians, can so conflate the two terms that not only the Christ but also Jesus himself becomes (quite ridiculously and improbably) pre-existent – a conflation which he also repeats in remarks on St John's gospel in the concluding chapter of his book:

> ... although Paul's notion of pre-existence is more implicit than explicit, it identifies a unique aspect of Jesus' sonship. Jesus was not merely exalted to, or adopted to, the status of being God's Son, he was God's Son previous to his resurrection, indeed, previous to his earthly existence ... Jesus enjoyed a unique status as God's Son since he was always the Son of God.
>
> ... it is Christ's status as God's pre-existent Son that endows his work with salvific value.[2]

If theologians can become so confused by the nature of the relationship between Jesus and the Christ, then what hope of properly distinguishing the identities of each is there for the rest of humanity?

But how easy and how tempting it is to conflate the two identities! Described as 'the greatest Jesus scholar of his generation', Geza Vermes makes this same crucial mistake, again in the context of St John's gospel: 'John's Jesus pre-existed in heaven.'[3] Indeed, even a theologian as distinguished as Karl Barth is to be found guilty on this count, as Karl-Josef Kuschel notes in his magisterial study exploring the origins of Christ:

> If we look closely, Barth takes the christology of pre-existence

to a speculative level which it had never reached in tradition in this form. For ... in the framework of his doctrine of election Barth taught an inclusion of the man Jesus in the pre-existence of the *Logos*, an identity of the incarnate Son with the pre-existent Son, of the ... Son become flesh with the eternal Son![4]

Kuschel himself is convinced that Barth is in error on this point, and he adduces the silence of both Jesus and his first disciples on this subject to support his argument. Of Jesus he says:

As far as we can tell on the basis of the New Testament, Jesus himself said nothing to indicate whether he thought himself to be the apocalyptic Son of Man/Messiah or had had a heavenly existence with God before time, a pre-existence before appearing on earth.[5]

The position is similar with regard to the disciples:

Nor did the first post-Easter community regard Jesus as the pre-existent Son of Man; they saw him as the eschatological Son of Man who was to come. If we suppose that the earliest community knew of the apocalyptic Son of Man tradition, this lack of interest in any kind of sayings about pre-existence, and even in any portrayal in a vision of a heavenly existence of Jesus before time, is striking.[6]

On these and various other grounds he concludes his discussion with a firm rebuttal of Barth's position:

There can be no question here [that is, in the Prologue to St John's gospel] of the pre-existence of the man Jesus, as Barth saw it. For exegetical reasons, objections must be made to Barth's christology of pre-existence and predestination.[7]

Nor is Kuschel alone in voicing this position, and indeed among modern christologists Barth would appear to be more or less in a minority of one. Thus one of the greatest of twentieth century christologists, John Macquarrie, writes, again of John's Prologue:

... I believe it [the Prologue] can be read in such a way that while it undoubtedly affirms that the *Logos* has existed 'from the beginning', this does not imply a personal pre-existence of Jesus Christ.[8]

And similarly, from a prominent Roman Catholic perspective, the eminent Jesuit theologian Gerald O'Collins has this to say:

> The human consciousness of Jesus did not pre-exist 'in heaven'. To claim that would be to threaten the genuineness of his humanity. The consciousness which did pre-exist was the divine consciousness of the eternal *Logos*, Wisdom, or Son of God. By assuming a full human existence and history, the person of the *Logos* came also to be known as Jesus of Nazareth and to be humanly conscious of himself.[9]

Admittedly all of these authors are writing from within the traditional framework of fixed ontology, and would argue that Jesus just was the Christ from the moment of birth or conception, but nonetheless their very clear separation of the persons of Jesus of Nazareth and the *Logos*/Word/Son of God opens up the way for a christology of becoming. Indeed, such a separation is essential. For were Jesus to be in any way the subject of pre-existence then this would settle once and for all any argument as to the necessity or contingency of the union between Jesus and the Christ: it would be, by definition, necessary. As we have seen, though, John's actual presentation of pre-existence is a good deal subtler than this and does not settle the issue of necessity or contingency one way or the other. We may still, if we wish, claim a necessary connection, but neither are we debarred from following through the ideas based on contingency which have been outlined here. The fourth evangelist might himself be surprised at such an approach, but his own theology by no means outlaws it.

The other significant feature about this Prologue – and indeed about all the books of the New Testament – is so patently obvious as to be hardly deserving of explicit mention, and yet it makes a profound difference to their interpretation, and this is simply that they were, necessarily, written retrospectively after the event and knowing the outcome. Thus there can hardly help but be a large degree of Barbara Tuchmann's outlawed 'flash-forwarding'. St John, like all of the other New Testament writers, is writing of a completed 'Christ-event' in which the union between Jesus and the Christ (regardless of how it came about) had been fully and immutably forged through death and resurrection. We may therefore readily concur with John's (and the New Testament as a whole's) conviction that Jesus is now indeed the Christ; but we may nonetheless legitimately argue on two grounds that this need not necessarily have been the case.

First, then, there is the embarrassingly frequent witness of the gospels themselves that during the human lifetime of Jesus this identification of him as the Christ was not anywhere near so consistently obvious as it later became. Jesus was not self-evidently and necessarily the Christ. Many times his own disciples reacted blindly to him and failed to respond adequately both to particular teachings and events and to the overall tenor and direction of his life towards Jerusalem and crucifixion. Indeed, even during his trial, by which time the process of becoming and the realisation of potential was well-nigh complete, the only reaction to any suggestion of union between Jesus and the Christ was one of 'Blasphemy!' Even as the union was being annealed in the furnace of death and subsequent resurrection, that same union was not universally recognised or even recognisable.

In this connection it is also worthy of note that according to the concensus of much of the best New Testament textual criticism, Jesus never – with the sole exception perhaps of at his trial – made this identification of himself with the Christ. It is as if this identification could not properly be made until it had become – or was at least by now bound to become – true. Indeed, the whole character of Jesus' ministry is, as we have attempted to demonstrate already, far more in keeping with the language of becoming than with a necessary and absolute identification. It is hard to imagine a Jesus who knew himself to be necessarily the Christ showing the hesitations about his own identity which we have previously discussed; and whether or not Jesus actually spoke them, those terrible words from the cross, 'My God, my God, why hast thou forsaken me?' reveal the Jesus of St Mark's gospel (and perhaps the Jesus of reality also) to be not a serene divinity assured of its eternal home, but a broken human being, afraid, even as union was being cemented by death, that it might all have been a frightful mistake or delusion.

The second point which needs to be made in connection with the retrospective nature of all of the New Testament scriptures, including St John's gospel, is that they are writing about Jesus as the Christ precisely and simply because this is what seemed overwhelmingly to them to have turned out to be the case, but this does not prevent us from suggesting that even though it was the case, it was not necessarily so. Had the story of Jesus turned out differently – as we have argued that it might at any one of many points have done – then the pre-existent Word would not have been proclaimed as dwelling perfectly in the man, Jesus.

There is now – and is now for all eternity – we believe, a proper identification of Jesus with the Christ, but this is due to an entirely contingent convergence between them which could, not only in principle, but also in reality, have been different. Jesus and the Christ are now for all eternity conjoined, but this does not have to mean that they have been so from all eternity in the fashion in which pre-existence is too easily, and mistakenly, understood. It is perfectly possible (as we have seen in our discussion of John 1:1-14) to posit a pre-existent Word – even conceived of as being in the relationship of the Son to the Father within an eternal Trinity – and also to hold that the incarnation of the Word/Son in Jesus is entirely contingent (rather than necessary) and conditional upon Jesus' continued 'Yes' rather than 'No' to the increasingly lonely and painful road of becoming. With Christians down the ages, I can read St John's Prologue with a profound conviction of its truth, the only difference (and yet, as we shall see, a far-reaching one) being that this conviction is tempered by an awed amazement that what actually happened might not have happened, and that our hope of redemption and eternal life through Jesus Christ came to us not out of philosophical or metaphysical necessity, but out of a continued act of divine call and a human response which did not have to happen.

If this line of approach is fruitful with regard to St John's Prologue, then a similar and equally fruitful approach is possible in response to the imagery of the cosmic Christ in the deutero-Pauline epistles to the Ephesians and the Colossians. We may rightly wish to see in Jesus Christ the 'image of the invisible God' and find in him the 'fullness' of divinity and all of the other ascriptions of these epistles, but none of this again precludes us from acknowledging this as an identity which has been written back only after the event (and which only then, indeed, became possible), and which could therefore have been different. There is, but there need not have been, anything either cosmic or Christly about Jesus of Nazareth. The pre-existence of the Word or the Son or the Christ is not incompatible with – and indeed appears to interact profoundly with – the becoming in time of the man Jesus as that Word, Son and Christ.

Notes
1. Rachel Feldhay Brenner, *Writing as Resistance: Four Women Confronting the Holocaust*, Pennsylvania, The Pennsylvania State University Press, 1997, p 67.
2. Frank J. Matera, *New Testament Christology*, Louisville & London, Westminster John Knox Press, 1999, p 106.
3. Geza Vermes, *Jesus: Nativity-Passion-Resurrection*, London, Penguin Books, 2010, p 364.
4. Karl-Joseph Kuschel, *Born Before All Time? The Dispute over Christ's Origin*, London, SCM Press, 1992, p 104.
5. Ibid, p 232.
6. Ibid.
7. Ibid, p 382.
8. John Macquarrie, *Jesus Christ in Modern Thought*, London and Philadelphia, SCM Press and Trinity Press International, 1990, p 389.
9. Gerald O'Collins SJ, *Christology: A Biblical, Historical and Systematic Study of Jesus*, Oxford, Oxford University Press, 1995, p 243.

CHAPTER SEVEN

One Christ or Many Christs?

At the close of the previous chapter it was commented that there need not have been anything cosmic or Christly about Jesus of Nazareth. The fact that there was and is, however, leads us back to the question and objection posed towards the end of Chapter Five: namely, if Jesus' realisation of potential and becoming led him to union with God, such that we now revere and worship him as God incarnate, then why, in principle, should this not be true of one or many others also, and what does this possibility infer about the uniqueness of Jesus and the Trinitarian nature of God? It is (although in a rather more serious vein) a little like the classic Monty Python sketch of many years ago, in which the Sistine Chapel rang to the pope's anguished cry of, 'Three Christs!'

As with our discussion of pre-existence, there are from the outset two possible approaches to the problem, one of which shirks the real nature of the challenge, and the other of which takes it more seriously. One answer to the problem, then, would be to adopt a thoroughly relativistic, broadly 'Sea of Faith' network attitude. This would allow one to sidestep the difficulties completely, since if God is only an idea or an ideal (or even the sum total of our ideals) then clearly there can be no objective content to the word 'God' and therefore no objective content either to the doctrine of the Trinity or the doctrine of the incarnation, and we are free to imagine or construct more or less any understanding of faith – whatever faith means from such a perspective – we may wish to choose. Here, as so often, though, relativism and non-objectivity fail to do justice to the truth claims and objective nature of the Christian faith as it has always been (and still is by the vast majority of believers) understood: it simply avers that these things no longer matter or that we have 'grown out' of them and now live in a spiritually autonomous and non-objective religious landscape. In the hands of someone as theologically skilled and literate as the Cambridge theologian Don Cupitt this can even be made to look, initially at least, like an attractive option, but all too often in other hands – including those of most of Cupitt's 'followers' who share his convictions but lack his theological acumen – it becomes full of theological contradictions and illogicalities and looks like an effort to take the intellectually easy way out by saying that some of the most central (and also the most intellectually difficult) concepts of Christianity are not worth dwelling on or wrestling with any longer. Relativism and non-objectivity all too easily become a thinly veiled excuse for intellectual and spiritual laziness: after all, if something doesn't exist or doesn't matter then what point is there in thinking about it at all?

In contrast to such an approach, we must, it seems to me, take seriously the truth claims and claims to objectivity made by the Christian faith as classically expressed, and as held throughout the ages. At one level, certainly, it is true that we can never know the truth about God, and indeed this whole area of human *agnosis* is one which I have discussed at considerable length in a previous volume.[1] For the present, suffice it to say that a finite human capacity for understanding can never, by definition, encompass divinity, and therefore all of our formulations about God, including Trinity and incarnation, will always only be partial approximations to reality which may or may not be more or less adequate in their depiction of that reality. At the same time, however, it is a central conviction of the Christian faith that however well or badly we may succeed in doing it, nonetheless there is a reality there to depict both in terms of God himself and in terms of his incarnation in Jesus Christ. Any re-thinking or change of emphasis within our faith must therefore reckon seriously with, and come to terms with such basic doctrinal convictions rather than simply dismiss them. In the case of an approach such as we are advocating here, we must acknowledge that there might at least appear to be potential contradictions involved regarding the uniqueness of Christ and the nature of the Trinity; and, just as with pre-existence, these apparent contradictions need to be resolved or explained before we can, with a good conscience as far as doctrine is concerned, proceed any further.

In relation to the doctrine of the Trinity, any apparent grounds for suspicion have largely been despatched already during the course of the discussion of pre-existence in the preceding chapter. In all essentials it makes no difference to our perception of God as Trinity whether incarnation at a particular time and place and in a particular individual is necessary or contingent, and indeed we have argued earlier that it is more in keeping with our general perception of God's nature and activity that it should be contingent. There is no intrinsic problem involved with the existence of a Son/Word out of time who becomes incarnate in time in a Jesus who himself becomes the Christ.

Potentially more serious is the issue of the uniqueness of Jesus as the Christ. According to any traditional metaphysical presentation of the incarnation, this presents no problem whatsoever. If incarnation was simply divinely willed as an absolute and therefore necessary fact, then Jesus is plainly unique, although I suppose it still remains logically possible (if unnecessary) that God might, for reasons of his own which we cannot fathom, wish to become incarnate again in another time and place – a possibility which Christianity has, rightly, never seriously entertained.

If, however, incarnation is understood according to the model advocated here, then at first sight the uniqueness of Jesus does not appear to be quite so closely safeguarded, for could not others potentially follow the same path of becoming as he did? And, in principle at least, if he became the Christ, then why not others?

This objection may perhaps best be countered on two grounds, and the result will be to leave us in what may well be an unfamiliar place, but one which will nonetheless turn out to be a thoroughly orthodox one. These grounds are first, what might be called the economy of salvation, and secondly (and ironically in view of the nature of the objection), the uniqueness of every human being, including, therefore, Jesus himself. Although these two areas are interlinked they are nonetheless separate, the first bearing largely on the activity of Jesus Christ (his doing), and the second being more concerned with the person and nature of Jesus Christ (his being).

First, then, what we might call the economy of salvation. Here we may begin from the – admittedly somewhat obvious – premise that the incarnation was an event with a *telos* or a purpose. The incarnation was not merely an exercise in God finding out for himself, as it were, what it feels like to be a human being; rather, the incarnation was a means to a very clearly defined end. There is no need here to rehearse the whole familiar doctrinal tale of fall and redemption: suffice it to say that Christianity has always seen humanity as being not only made in the 'image and likeness' of God, but also, tragically, through sin and disobedience, separated from God. At the very heart of our faith, therefore, is the conviction and consequent proclamation that this separation is once and for all overcome in and through the life, death and resurrection of Jesus Christ. Admittedly there are numerous theories of atonement, some more satisfactory than others, but no matter which theory is espoused this is the central truth at issue. The 'how' of the atonement – how Jesus' life and death reconcile us with God – may receive a wide variety of different answers; but the 'what' of the atonement – what it is, by whatever means, that this life and death achieve – is consistently proclaimed to be reconciliation with God leading to the promise of salvation and eternal life.

The ending of the separation between ourselves and God was, therefore, the task and the purpose of the incarnation, and in Jesus Christ this purpose has been for once and for all achieved. It is not a task which need ever be – or indeed ever could be – repeated for, if we are as we believe now reconciled to God, then there is clearly no need for any further such reconciling action. It follows logically, therefore, that if the accomplishment of this task was (and eternally is) achieved through the becoming in time of Jesus as the Christ, then there is no place for any second or subsequent Christ-figures. Humanity and divinity have already met and joined for all time and for all people in the Christ-ship of Jesus and there is no need – or place – for precise repetition – although there is, as we shall see later, most certainly a place for other lives of reconciliation. The becoming of Jesus to be the Christ was a specific vocation for a specific purpose, which, once achieved, is, and remains ever, unique.

At this point in the argument it is essential to counter one further potential criticism of a christology of becoming, which, if it is a valid criticism, is alone enough to vitiate any possible arguments in favour of such a christology. Thus, put at its plainest, a Christology of becoming would appear, at first sight at least, to lay itself open to the charge of Pelagianism – and worse.

Stated at its briefest, the Pelagian heresy argued that human nature was genuinely and absolutely free to respond to God and to choose the good in and of itself. Such a view was entirely contrary to the prevailing Augustinian doctrine that humanity was so sunk in sin that its will was not genuinely free to seek the good, and that, unaided, human nature could only ever fail to reach it. Attaining both good and God depended entirely upon co-operating with the grace of God, and particularly upon being the recipient of God's 'prevenient' grace – that is, a grace which goes before us and is received prior to ever asking for it, such that henceforward we are more disposed to respond to the more overt manifestations of co-operative grace.

In the context of the present discussion, the potential charge is two-fold: first, are we not presenting Jesus as the arch-Pelagian (albeit before Pelagius!), a human being 'proving' that human nature can indeed perform the celebrated 'boot-strap' trick and, effectively, work out its own salvation; and secondly, if Jesus can do this, then why cannot anyone (or everyone) else, and is incarnation, therefore, actually not necessary to salvation after all? These are weighty charges, and they deserve our careful attention.

First, then, the issue of a Pelagian redeemer. Effectively the rationale for combating this accusation has already been given in Chapter Two, but one or two connections need here to be spelt out more fully in order to clarify the nature of the defence. It is important to grasp, then, the underlying reasons for Augustine's rejection of Pelagius' position. These were, as we have seen in Chapter Two, his innate convictions (stemming from his own personality and past as much as from anything else) first, of original sin, and secondly of a concomitant original guilt. It is these things, he argues, which vitiate any hope of a truly free will for humanity. Already, in that same chapter, though, we have argued the necessity for a major revision of Augustine's doctrine of original sin, and that argument reaches perhaps its full force in the present context. If, as I believe, Augustine was simply wrong in his assertion of original sin and associated original guilt, then, as Pelagius asserted, there is indeed no reason why human nature should not be able to choose the path of goodness and Godliness at any and every turn. In fact, the biggest problem is one of fear: Pelagius has been consigned to the sin bin of history, and orthodoxy has a way of throwing up its hands in genteel horror whenever his name is mentioned. The simple fact is, though, that Augustine was utterly and disastrously wrong, and this being so one may, with a good theological conscience, rescue some of the best of Pelagius' ideas, and not least the notion that humanity is a great deal more capable of freely choosing both good and God than Augustine could ever have imagined. And this does not mean that Jesus has performed any 'boot-strap' trick. Humanity (even in Jesus Christ) has not saved itself: it has been saved by God precisely in and through its own freely chosen co-operation with the grace, might and love of God himself. God remains firmly the author of our salvation, and humanity's part, in the person of Jesus of Nazareth, is one of actively choosing to be the parchment upon which the text of salvation is inscribed by that divine author.

This insistence upon the grace of God and Jesus' freely chosen co-operation with it also largely answers therefore the second part of this current objection: that of the necessity or otherwise of the incarnation to salvation. For God's way with humanity, from the beginning of the Old Testament onwards, is one of covenant, of partnership, of mutual responsibility and obligation. Admittedly the actual term covenant is not always used, but that (or something very like it) is always the underlying relationship: with Adam and Eve, with Noah, with Abraham, Isaac and Jacob, with Moses, with kings and prophets and so on. Always there is an inherent element of mutuality in the relationship between God and his people: God does not simply act regardless of his people, but rather they must behave in such a way that God's action on their behalf is, if not entirely merited, at least drawn forth in response to their good faith in both will and action.

This being the case, would it not be odd, and – if the phrase is admissible when applied to God – out of character if God were to work the most wonderful of all his works in a non-covenantal manner: if forgiveness and eternal salvation were to be unilaterally bestowed by divine fiat regardless of the actions and wills of the entirety of humanity? Surely it is in keeping with the revealed activity of God that human co-operation should, at some level, be required in the redemption of humanity.

If this assessment of God's activity is accurate, as I believe it is, then incarnation remains essential to salvation. For if God is to continue to work in partnership, or even covenant, with the human race, then incarnation is vital, since if salvation was to be achieved for all, then someone, on behalf of that all, had to fulfil this vocation of becoming in the name of all those who could not achieve it for themselves – and this becoming was perfected precisely in the person of Jesus of Nazareth. Only through incarnation could humanity assume divinity and divinity redeem humanity. Redemption became reality when God took into himself and justified, by resurrection and ascension, the human being Jesus of Nazareth. Without that taking of humanity into divinity (expressed in traditional theology as divinity 'assuming' humanity) there can be no salvation. Redemption still depends upon the incarnation, even in this contingent and becoming mode, for incarnation still remains the bridge, or even better, the meeting place, between God and humanity, heaven and earth.

At this point, having warded off the potential charges of heresy, and established once again the necessity of incarnation, we must return to the main argument of this chapter concerning the uniqueness of Jesus Christ, and address one further subsidiary question. Thus earlier on in this chapter we may have ruled out the possibility of further Christs, but we have not as yet addressed the issue of the potential of other human beings to 'equal' Jesus' constant choosing and obedience and sinlessness. It may well never have happened, for Jesus is the only person of whom the Christian tradition does actually predicate sinlessness and perfect obedience, but the possibility nonetheless remains, even if not for the past, at least for the future. A second Christ there may not be, but a second perfection there may, in theory, possibly be – and what of such a possibility?

I propose to explore the possibilities open to human nature

more fully in the next chapter, in the course of illustrating how a christology of becoming might actually work, but here we are concerned solely with the issue of Christ's uniqueness. In essence the answer to the question of a second perfection is the same both for the holy (if ultimately imperfect) figures of the past, and for any putative example(s) of future perfection, and this answer lies precisely and orthodoxly in the achievement of Jesus as the Christ. Very simply, all of these other figures, whether past, present or future, were or are not called to become Christs, but rather to respond to the Christ, and in that response to imitate, as nearly as may be, his perfection. Their participation in divinity (and that of the rest of us also) is now through Jesus Christ, and does not depend upon all (or any) of the rest of humanity striving to become further Christs – except, of course, in so far as in the imitation of him we do seek to become the medium of Christ's enduring presence here on earth. The approach may be very different from that of classical metaphysics, but the 'once for all' nature of Christ and of our redemption is no less firmly safeguarded for that.

The second answer to the objection which this chapter seeks to address is closely related to – although subtly different from – the uniqueness of the Christ-ship of Jesus explored above. This is simply the uniqueness, both in character, gifts and so on, and in calling or vocation, of every human being, Jesus, of course, included.

This claim of uniqueness is so obvious as scarcely to need mentioning, but it is nonetheless material to the argument at this point. Thus every human being is unique. Each person is uniquely him or her self. On a purely physical level this is self-evident, and such things as DNA and finger-prints bear eloquent testimony to it. Similarly, although less scientifically, we know it for ourselves. We recognise the uniqueness of each individual: by their looks, manner, voice and so on. We know that we are talking to Jean and not Jane, Jack and not John.

Furthermore, what is true of the physical level is equally true on the more psychological levels of spirit, character and abilities. Each of has a unique and therefore different make up as well as gifts and abilities to bring to our common world. We may be predominantly practical or intellectual, extrovert or

introvert, flower-arranger, musician, author, carpenter, or whatever. The range of possibilities and combinations is, almost literally, endless, and each of us reflects one particular sparkling
facet of the prism of human potential. With our own especial
gifts and character we are all called to be uniquely ourselves,
and if we are asked any questions on judgement day, the question will not be why were we not all like Jesus, but why were we
not fully and perfectly ourselves as we were created to be, and
as Jesus was fully and perfectly himself.[2]

Going even one stage further, from physique to character,
and now to vocation, if it is true that we are unique in the first
and second of these categories, then why not also in the third –
vocation? Thus each of us has a specific calling to be and to do
something which no-one else has been asked to be and do, and
which is therefore every bit as unique as our physical features
and our character. Beethoven was not called to be a second
Mozart, nor Charlotte Bronte to be a second Jane Austen: they
were called to be themselves and to fulfil their own singular and
unique vocation. And so too, by definition, with Jesus of
Nazareth. He was called to become the Christ, and that being so,
that calling is, equally by definition, unique. There can be and
will be no others, and the calling of all who would follow him is
that of 'imitatio Christi' rather than 'replicatio Christi'.

Finally, having disposed of the spectre of the Sistine Chapel's
'Three Christs!' it is worth noting that this argument from
uniqueness – both that of Jesus himself and that of every human
being – and, indeed, the whole notion of a christology of becoming, is theologically very much in line with two thoroughly biblical christological insights.

The first of these is St Paul's 'old and new Adam' typology as
outlined in such passages as 1 Corinthians 15:45-49 and Romans
5:12-19. The whole of this typology is built upon the contrast between Adam's fatal disobedience and the absolute and life-giv-
ing obedience of Jesus. In becoming the Christ in the way in
which we have outlined here, Jesus reveals a uniquely perfect
obedience to God. A philosophically necessary connection (such
as has always been assumed in traditional christology) between
Jesus and the Christ entirely negates the value of any supposed
obedience, since in this scenario the man Jesus of Nazareth has,

by definition, no real choice in the matter, and what can the concept of obedience possibly mean then? It is, ironically, in view of the fact that it undoes so much of classical christology, only if we accept a purely contingent connection between Jesus and the Christ, that this deeply biblical christological thread actually acquires any real meaning in the context of contemporary christology.

The other biblical insight is, as we have explored earlier, St John's poetic reflection on (amongst other things) pre-existence in the Prologue to his gospel, and this firmly underpins our own affirmation of the uniqueness of the incarnation. Again it is the obedience, choosing and constant becoming which bring Jesus of Nazareth into total union with the pre-existent Word or Christ, and this is a unique vocation which can never be repeated, but remains a once-for-all event, but one in which all now participate. It appears that by means which are far from the premises of classical theology, we have arrived at an almost startlingly orthodox position.

In the course of the last few chapters we have, in reaching this position, explored in some depth the nature of God and the nature of incarnation. However, before we can proceed to consider the wider implications of a theology of becoming for the areas of doctrine, ecclesiology and ethics, there is one further consideration to be addressed: human nature. We have established that God is not compromised by a christology of becoming, but we need to revisit from a different angle some of the territory explored in Chapter Two, and ask whether human nature (aside from questions of original sin and original guilt which were dealt with there) is actually capable of becoming or assuming divinity.

Notes
1. For a fuller treatment of this issue, see: Stephen R. White, *A Space for Unknowing: The Place of Agnosis in Faith*, Dublin, Columba Press, 2006. See also Stephen R. White, 'Agnosticism' in *The Cambridge Dictionary of Christian Theology*, Ian A. McFarland, David A. S. Fergusson, Karen Kilby and Iain R. Torrance (eds), Cambridge, CUP, 2011.
2. This question is an old Jewish one which was given its classical formulation by Rabbi Zusya: 'In the world to come, I will not be asked, why weren't you Moses? I will be asked, why weren't you Zusya?'

CHAPTER EIGHT

Ecce Homo Sapiens

In posing the question of whether humanity is capable of, as it were, bearing the burden of divinity, we have asked a question which is, from a traditional christological perspective, quite obviously a non-question, for the answer is a simple 'Yes'. But it is only so because of the failings of this traditional approach to which we have referred previously. That is, any christology which pre-supposes a necessary connection between Jesus and the Christ automatically, and by definition – even if it strenuously denies it – plays down the full humanity of Jesus Christ. It does so because the union between humanity and divinity does not ultimately depend upon the man, Jesus, but upon the miraculous activity of God in assuming humanity through the Virgin Birth and so on.

Furthermore, this traditional account of incarnation in fact downplays the significance of humanity implicitly even more than it does explicitly. For in spite of the even-handedness of the terminology used, the actual impression gained from any traditional christology – its sub-text, if you like – is not so much that divinity assumed humanity as that humanity was subsumed in divinity. In fact, the real question posed by such christologies is not the question of whether human nature can bear the weight of divinity, but whether the nature which does so in Jesus is, in reality, fully and authentically human at all points.

In a christology of becoming, the reality of the human nature involved is not at issue, but the question of the ability of human nature to attain total union with God – sidestepped by all of the usual christological methods – raises itself with some force and demands our sustained attention here.

An obvious starting-point is to return to the creation of humanity in the 'image and likeness' of God which was touched upon in Chapter Four. Here, as there, the precise distinctions of meaning between the two terms is not at issue. What is at issue is the fact that taken together they point to the idea that there is no complete disjunction between our human nature and the nature of God. The implication is that there may be, or even must be, certain ways in which human nature bears within itself the stamp of the divine, and therefore the possibility of union with the divine nature.

Plainly there are certain divine attributes which humanity cannot share, simply because it is temporal and not eternal. It is not open to any human being to become, for example, omniscient or omnipotent as we believe God to be. But are these really the most significant defining qualities of God, or do they not rather just 'go with the territory', as it were? For surely it would be possible to imagine a God who is indeed omniscient and omnipotent, but also vengeful, cruel and hard-hearted. Omniscience, omnipotence and the like are metaphysical qualities which have, in themselves, no moral value or, indeed, ethical overtones whatsoever, and it is surely, principally in the revealed will and moral nature of God that the most essential aspects of divinity must be presumed to reside.

On this far more significant level, God has consistently revealed himself as having a very particular will and 'character', witnessed to in commandments, codes of conduct, the writings of the prophets and so on. It would be tedious in the extreme to trawl right through the Old Testament for examples of this will and 'character'. Suffice it to say that the overriding testimony is to a God of faithfulness, compassion, mercy and love, and a God who demands these qualities of his people such that they act as he acts: to leap forward to the New Testament for a moment, 'Be ye therefore perfect as your heavenly Father is perfect' (Matthew 5:48). And these qualities and others like them are not beyond the grasp of humanity: they do not depend upon eternity, but are quite capable of being realised temporally. Admittedly the record of the human race in this respect is not particularly good, but the actual outcome does not undermine the possibilities inherent in being human. In principle it remains possible for a human being to think, speak and act in perfect harmony with this revealed will and character of God and so partake of that same divine nature.

This is an insight which has not been lost on a variety of theologians, especially during the mid to late twentieth century, and so it is all the more surprising that, as far as I am aware, none of them has as yet departed from traditional metaphysical categories of thought in dealing with the incarnation and gone on to develop a christology of becoming such as has been outlined here. The seeds of this notion that humanity has a divine potential were, for the modern era at least, sown in the early nineteenth century by Schleiermacher in his *magnum opus, The Christian Faith*, first published in 1821 and then re-published in a much-revised second edition in 1830. In the course of affirming the full humanity of Jesus he comments almost casually – but also momentously:

> As certainly as Christ was a man, there must reside in human nature the possibility of taking up the divine into itself, just as did happen in Christ.[1]

The existence of this possibility has been echoed by several major theologians during more recent decades. Thus, writing over 150 years later in 1990, John Macquarrie, one of the finest christologists of the twentieth century, quotes Schleiermacher approvingly and adds:

> ... I think he [Schleiermacher] was right in claiming that what we may call a union with the divine was possible for Jesus of Nazareth only because this is a potency that is present in all human nature.[2]

Others may not refer directly to Schleiermacher as Macquarrie does, but the same underlying conviction of the potential of human nature for union with the divine is there nonetheless. Probably the finest recent survey of modern christology (in this case specifically Anglican christology) is the Irish Roman Catholic Niall Coll's *Christ in Eternity and Time*, and in the course of this he remarks not only on Macquarrie but also on Eric Mascall, for whom he says: '... human nature, as created, possesses a passive fitness (*potential obedientialis*) for *hypostatic union* with God.'[3]

But it is not merely British or Anglican theologians who share this conviction of human potential. Such an iconic figure as Karl Rahner is similarly persuaded, as Karl-Josel Kuschel demonstrates in an incisive overview of Rahner's christology:

> ... for Rahner, God's becoming man is not something miraculous or mythological which once took place in a man in a remote period but is bound up with human possibilities generally, if not necessarily given with them. In Jesus Christ there has appeared what is present as an innermost possibility in any human being (the God-manhood of human beings), but was realised definitively in Jesus Christ. Only in Jesus Christ does there come together what is always already pre-supposed in principle in all human beings, in their striving for meaning, hoping, longing, persevering, indeed in the process of the self-transcendence of the world generally: God's definitive turning towards the world and human beings on the one hand, and the complete and final acceptance of God's promise of himself through human beings in free obedience on the other.[4]

The potential of humanity for union with divinity (without any need for metaphysical sleight of hand to make it work) is, it now appears, no stranger to theology in the modern period.

But even allowing for the possibility – as it now appears that we must – that humanity does possess this potential, a second issue now arises. That is, if we are going to dispense with traditional metaphysical categories (*persona, hypostasis* and the like) then how are we now going to endeavour to express the manner in which this union takes place? That it may take place has been established; how it may take place has yet to be explored.

We may perhaps begin from the premise that this union can only possibly occur when whatever aspects there may be of human nature which would impede it have been sloughed off. And the facet of human nature which is most resistant to such union – as it is resistant to any contact which threatens its own centrality – is the ego. By this I do not mean merely a sense of self, and nor do I employ it as a technical psychological term in the manner of Freud. Rather, I mean that ever-present tendency in human nature which wants to place 'me' at the centre of things, and which may issue in self-importance, selfishness, the putting-down or ignoring of others and other such destructive behaviours.

We see, from time to time, in the people around us, to what a shining degree this can be done: all of us have met people who seem to exist only in so far as they are there for other people. They do not have to be famous like St Francis of Assisi or Mother Teresa of Calcutta: I think immediately of the then Principal of my theological college. Nor does the banishment of the ego diminish character, although it does, of course, transform it. And it does so precisely by the development of a quality of attention to the 'other', whose needs, fears and hopes are of equal importance to my own.

This quality of attention to the other has been singled out as the ultimate hallmark of goodness by moral philosophers such as Simone Weil and Iris Murdoch. Murdoch, in particular, stresses the relationship of attention to moral goodness, although she also readily admits her indebtedness to Simone Weil:

> I have used the word 'attention', which I borrow from Simone Weil, to express the idea of a just and loving gaze directed upon an individual reality. I believe this to be the characteristic and proper mark of the active moral agent.[5]

Furthermore, she clearly equates this depth of attention with the quality of love: 'The direction of attention is, contrary to nature, outward, away from self [...] and the ability so to direct attention is love'.[6] Murdoch, of course, writes from an a-theistic perspective, but the concept of 'attention' remains equally valid in a theistic context. Thus, from a religious perspective we may say that this equates with the second of the two great commandments: 'Love your neighbour as yourself.'

Up to this point, it may be argued, what has been achieved may remain a purely secular goodness which does not require any acknowledgement of God at all, and indeed all of us will have known people with no religious affiliation or conviction whatsoever, but who nonetheless forcefully and unequivocally strike us as 'good'. But this same process of the de-centring of the ego may also lead us (although admittedly it does not have to) towards the realisation of the fulfilment of the first great commandment: 'You shall love the Lord your God with all your heart and with all your soul and with all your mind.'

Granted, for most of us our attempts to love God in such a way are sporadic and half-hearted, and the 'fat relentless ego'[7] regularly intrudes to cast its distorted and distorting shadow between ourselves and God. But our many (and all too real) failures in this regard do not vitiate the possibility of a genuine egoless and open full attention to God. Even leaving Jesus to one side for a brief moment, we see at least something of this kind in the lives of the saints. There is a story (probably, admittedly, apocryphal) of a child who was asked in a Sunday School class to define a saint. Thinking of the familiar figures in the church's stained glass windows, the child instantly replied: 'A saint is someone who the light shines through.' And this, it seems to me, is a wonderful image of this process of unselfing and opening oneself to God at work. It is as if the more we can put the ego and its selfish wants to one side and the more we can thereby be open to God, then the more fully are God's light, grace, love and will able to dwell within us and be reflected through us.

Such a divine indwelling and reflection is emphatically possible, as is witnessed to not only in the lives of the canonical saints but in the everyday saints whom we all encounter at various points in our own lives and at whose goodness and holiness we can only marvel. Why, in principle, then, might it not be possible for this indwelling and reflection of divinity to be so complete and perfect that humanity and divinity are at last in union, humanity raised into divinity, divinity kenotically assuming humanity? And surely it is precisely this, though here shorn of all Greek and Latin metaphysical terms and concepts, which we affirm to have definitively taken place in the incarnation. We do not need metaphysics or an opposition between above and below christologies (all things which only get in the way anyway) in order to forge a coherent and contemporarily relevant and understandable model of the incarnation, in which God is seen as fulfilling the ultimate potential of humanity which now, in Jesus of Nazareth, is not only in his 'image and likeness' but shares in his very nature.

I have commented earlier that no-one, as far as I know, has hitherto thoroughly explored the possibility of a christology of becoming, but this does not mean that no-one has – quite possibly unknowingly – opened up a space for such a possibility.

Two contemporary theologians in particular seem to me between them to allow for just such an understanding of christology as is developed here. These are Stanley Hauerwas and
James P. Mackey. Thus Hauerwas is convinced that christology
is rooted at least as much in humanity as in divinity:

> ... it became clear to me that questions surrounding how to
> understand the person and work of Christ are integrally re-
> lated to our understanding of what it means for us to be
> human.[8]

Mackey would concur with this, and in a passage deserving of
lengthy quotation he outlines just such an outpouring of divinity into an open, ego-free and attending humanity as I have delineated in this chapter:

> ... all talk of the divinity of Jesus really has to do with a pres-
> ence of God in Jesus, 'reconciling the world to himself,' as
> Paul ... somewhere put it. It has to do with the degree of that
> divine presence in Jesus, and that degree in turn depends
> upon the degree of self-emptying by Jesus of all purely self-
> ish regard and aim, so that he should prove an absolutely un-
> hindered and uncluttered channel of divine creative power
> in creation.[9]

And similarly, whilst interestingly also echoing my own feel-
ings as to the contemporary unintelligibility and therefore re-
dundancy of so much of classical metaphysics:

> ... all statements about the divinity of Jesus should be so
> fashioned and expressed as to let it be clearly understood
> that the reference is not to the divinity *of* Jesus, but to the di-
> vinity *in* Jesus; so permanently, powerfully and unobstruct-
> edly present in Jesus that everything human that the fully
> human Jesus did and said and thought became the very
> model – sometimes, admittedly, after a bit of a struggle – of
> the eternal creative-salvific activity of God's own self in the
> world. This is what the ancient Council of Chalcedon tried to
> express in what have long become the commonly unintelligi-
> ble metaphysical concepts of Greek philosophy: a divine and
> a human nature operated on creation through the one person
> of Jesus of Nazareth, the latter ever freely providing the

fleshly forms of thoughts, words and actions, while freely re-
moving any impediments to the flow and direction of the indwelling divine Spirit/Word that in-breathed his whole life;
the former being as fully and truly divine as the latter was
fully and truly human.[10]

And, of course, in addition to these two distinguished figures,
we have also the testimony of Schleiermacher, Macquarrie and
Rahner adduced earlier in this chapter.

It appears, then, that a christology of becoming, although not
previously voiced entirely or explicitly, is a theologically respectable position which is consonant with insights garnered
from the Christian theological tradition. Even more compellingly
than this, though, such a christology actually appears authentically to reflect the belief of the earliest Christian communities, a
belief which was rapidly smothered under the weight of metaphysics during the centuries of the patristic era. Earlier in this
study we have already discussed the opening of St Paul's letter
to the Romans ('descended from Joseph according to the flesh
and designated Son of God in power according to the Spirit of
holiness by his resurrection from the dead'), but this understanding of christology belongs not only to St Paul, but also, and
vitally, to the earliest preaching of the apostles themselves. Thus
Peter, in his 'sermon' on the Day of Pentecost says:

> This Jesus God raised up, and of that we are all witnesses.
> Being therefore exalted at the right hand of God, and having
> received from the Father the promise of the Holy Spirit, he
> has poured out his which you see and hear. For David did
> not ascend into the heavens; but he himself says, 'The Lord
> said to my Lord, Sit at my right hand, till I make thy enemies
> a stool for thy feet.' Let all the house of Israel therefore know
> assuredly that God has made him both Lord and Christ, this
> Jesus whom you crucified.

Peter clearly envisages Jesus as being appointed to his Messianic
office, just as St Paul understands him as being 'designated' to
receive his Sonship. In a compelling analysis of this passage,
Karl-Josef Kuschel outlines the significance of this understanding, and, interestingly, also links it (as we have here) with St
Paul's interpretation of Jesus:

What did belief in the resurrection of Jesus involve? Against the background of Jewish tradition, evidently the belief not just that a dead man had escaped death, but rather that this crucified man had been exalted and enthroned beside God, i.e. had been appointed to his messianic office. This at any rate is the way in which the Acts of the Apostles understood the resurrection, and it has preserved this understanding in the first sermon of Peter after Pentecost. This is a text which despite Lukan revision still clearly shows elements of old notions which go back to the Jerusalem community ... And the same level of tradition may also have contained the christological opening that Paul uses for his letter to the Romans, in which this early christology, still firmly rooted in the sphere of Jewish thought, will have found its classical expression.[11]

A christology of becoming, then, far from being a departure from orthodoxy, would seem to be not only in keeping with the possibilities inherent in human nature, but also a recovery of the convictions of the earliest Christians regarding the Jesus whom they had known when alive and whom they then experienced afresh as resurrected to become Messiah and Son of God.

As we will see in the succeeding chapters, the recovery of such a christology has implications for a variety of other areas of theology, but there is one immediate implication for ourselves and our own human nature which we need at least briefly to touch upon here. This is, quite simply but stupendously, the new vision and new possibilities which are opened up for us by such a christology.

In an earlier chapter we have discussed the age-old christological distinction of whether Jesus is different from us in degree or in kind. There we argued that these are not necessarily the only categories through which we may approach christology, but here their relevance is the effect which either of them has upon our perception of ourselves as followers of Jesus Christ. Plainly a difference of kind places an immediate qualitative distinction between Jesus and the whole of humanity. He is, as it were, a 'one-off' in terms of his nature, and we can never aspire to be 'as he is', but only followers stumbling in his wake with no hope of ever becoming like him by nature.

Degree christologies are obviously less absolute in their basic premise. However, if one wishes to remain within the fold of orthodoxy and avoid a descent into something like a kind of modern-day Arianism, then the degree involved must be so great as to create a gulf between us almost as vast as that created by christologies founded upon a difference in kind.

This gulf is removed if we ignore the old christologies of degree and kind and work with the model of a christology of becoming. For if, in Jesus, humanity could open itself to a complete indwelling by God, then there is, in principle, no reason why this should not be a possibility for any or all of the rest of us also. For the first time a genuine possibility of *imitatio Christi* is opened up to us, and what a difference that might make to our sense of Christian vocation. It does not mean, as we discussed in Chapter Seven that there may be further Christs: that was one very specific vocation fulfilled once and for all in and by Jesus of Nazareth. But it does mean that we, as his followers, are now genuinely empowered with the potential to be authentically his hands and his feet on earth and the channels of his redeeming love. The beautiful meditation of St Teresa of Avila takes on a new life and a new resonance:

> Christ has now no body on earth but yours,
> No hands but yours, no feet but yours;
> Yours are the eyes through which must look out
> Christ's compassion on the world.
> Yours are the feet with which
> He is to go about doing good.
> Yours are the hands with which
> He is to bless people now.

This, at last, can ring true not merely as Christian aspiration, but as reality in daily lived Christian experience.

Once again we may return to one of the finest contemporary christologists, James P. Mackey, for confirmation as to the validity (and wonder) of this new perspective on our vocation as Christians. Although, as we have seen, Mackey makes a space for it, he does not spell out a christology of becoming, but he does articulate the heightened perception of vocation which such a christology would bring:

... Jesus was son of God also in the sense that he was Saviour.
As could we too be, derivatively, sons and daughters of God
and auxiliary saviours, if we dined and healed like he did.
For the healings and the meals are both and equally saving
processes, salvation activities ...

Feeding to people the necessities and enhancements of
life exemplified in food clearly makes them well, as does
healing their life-diminishing ills, while simultaneously
breathing into them, one hopes, the spirit in which the mutual
feeding and the healing is done, and thereby inducing a
change of heart or spirit, the *metanoia* that is too often translated as repentance. In fact it is that latter effect of the feed-
ings and the healings that is by far the more salvific, and that
makes the ones who engage in the dining and healing all the
more effective as saviours who make all well and all manner
of thing well.[12]

Contrary to St Augustine, then, with whom we took issue in an
earlier chapter, humanity, for all of its real and obvious faults,
may, in its essential nature, be construed not as a *massa damnata*
but rather as a *massa beata*, for it is that for which it was created
in the 'image and likeness' of God and which therefore represents also its true *telos* or purpose.

Throughout the first part of this study we have concentrated
on what I have called the 'possibility of becoming' and established the theological and biblical credentials for such a position.
We have seen that it does not jeopardise the uniqueness of Jesus
and that it would appear to be in keeping both with our understanding of God and with our understanding of ourselves. It remains, though, to establish what we might call the 'benefits of becoming': in other words, what positive and beneficial consequences might ensue for other areas of Christian doctrine and
practice if such a view of christology were to gain widespread acceptance within the life of the church. It is the nature of these benefits which will form the substance of Part Two of this volume.

Notes

1. Frederick Schleiermacher, *The Christian Faith*, English Translation, Edinburgh, T & T Clark, 1928, p 64.

2. John Macquarrie, *Jesus Christ in Modern Thought*, London and Philadelphia, SCM Press and Trinity Press International, 1990, p 203.

3. Niall Coll, *Christ in Eternity and Time: Modern Anglican Perspectives*, Dublin, Four Courts Press, 2001, p 69.

4. Karl-Josef Kuschel, *Born Before All Time? The Dispute over Christ's Origin*, London, SCM Press, 1992, p 414.

5. Iris Murdoch, 'The Idea of Perfection', in *Existentialists and Mystics*, London, Chatto & Windus, Date?, pp 299-336, p 327.

6. Iris Murdoch, 'On 'God' and 'Good'', in *Existentialists and Mystics*, pp 337-62, p 354.

7. Iris Murdoch, 'On 'God' and 'Good'', in *Existentialists and Mystics*, pp 337-62, p 342.

8. Stanley Hauerwas, *Hannah's Child: A Theologian's Memoir*, London, SCM Press, 2010, pp 52-3.

9. James P. Mackey, *Jesus of Nazareth: The Life, the Faith and the Future of the Prophet (A Brief History)*, Dublin, The Columba Press, 2008, p 229.

10. Ibid.

11. Kuschel, p 227.

12. Mackey, p 151.

PART TWO

The Benefits of Becoming

CHAPTER NINE

The Simple Truth

The history of Christian theology has a lot to answer for, not least as a result of the fact that the doctrinal accretions of successive centuries have burdened Christianity with an almost impossibly convoluted and over-precise and over-literal system of beliefs. We have already discussed the damage done to Christianity by its thraldom to metaphysics and philosophy, but here we turn to a doctrine which, being scriptural, has in one sense been there from the beginning, but which has been corrupted through its exposure to the rigid systematising tendencies of the early centuries of doctrinal debate. In approaching it we will re-visit some of the territory explored in Chapters One and Two. There we examined the supposed need to safeguard the divinity of Jesus from fallen humanity: here, we shall argue that the doctrine in its literal form is logically redundant and should remain as symbol only. The doctrine in question is that of the Virginal Conception of Jesus, more commonly but less accurately known as the Virgin Birth – and with it, though held only by the Roman Catholic Church and only promulgated very much later, the doctrine of the Immaculate Conception.

The doctrine of the Virginal Conception of Jesus is rooted in only two of the four gospels (those of Matthew and Luke) and is known nowhere else in scripture, a fact eloquently delineated by Geza Vermes:

> This dogma is exclusively based on a few verses of the infancy gospels; no other section of the New Testament inside or outside the gospels makes any reference to it either explicitly or even implicitly.[1]

It received much of its historical importance thanks to the development by St Augustine of the doctrines of original sin and concomitant original guilt, the rationale of this being, as we saw earlier, that Jesus' virginal conception removes him from the realm of tainted humanity and thereby allows for an absolute perfection which is not available to anyone who has the misfortune to be conceived in the normal way.

There are a number of problems with this doctrine, and likewise a number of good reasons for seeking to dislodge it – in its literal form at least. To begin with there is a straightforward textual problem with Matthew's account (although admittedly not with Luke's) in that Matthew's insistence on the virginity of Mary rests at least in part on a mistranslation of a key passage in the Septuagint, the *koine* Greek version of the Jewish Bible (our Old Testament) with which the author of Matthew would have been familiar.

Throughout his gospel Matthew is keen to present Jesus as the fulfiller of prophecy. Many references are made to the writing prophets of the Old Testament, and it is Matthew who uses, in the Sermon on the Mount, the telling construction, 'You have heard that it was said to those of ancient times … But I say to you …' For Matthew, Old Testament events and prophecies look forward to Jesus as the one who is to come. It is hardly surprising, therefore, to find him using this technique in connection with the birth of Jesus. He quotes Isaiah 7:14: 'Look, the virgin shall conceive and bear a son, and they shall name him Emmanuel.' Unfortunately for Matthew's case, however, the word 'virgin' in the Septuagint is a mistranslation of the original Hebrew text which reads simply, 'young woman'. We have no means of accurately assessing Matthew's thought process, and we therefore cannot tell whether he is citing Isaiah as 'proof' of Jesus' virginal conception and the idea of such a conception has come from another independent source of tradition, or whether he is using this verse from Isaiah to argue that as Jesus is its fulfiller he must therefore have been virginally conceived. Either way, however, the text sits uneasily, and permanently threatens to bear a contrary witness to Jesus' conception from the one which Matthew himself intended it to bear.

The other major problem with this doctrine is that it is no more intrinsically believable than any of the other stories of virginal conception which occur in a variety of Greek, Roman and Near-Eastern religions of the time. Certainly the 'official' church

line in all denominations has been to endorse the historicity of
the doctrine, but equally, at least since the Enlightenment, in-
creasing numbers of reputable theologians have shed more than
a little doubt on it. Thus, no less a figure than Hans Küng observed in his *magnum opus, On Being a Christian*:

> Although the virgin birth cannot be understood as a histori-
> cal-biological event, it can be regarded as a meaningful sym-
> bol at least for that time.[2]

Even more bluntly, James P. Mackey argues cogently in a discussion of St John's gospel:

> ... as his [Jesus'] puzzled and alienated listeners in John 6
> quite reasonably observe, they know very well where he
> came from – from the very earthly seed of Joseph and the
> womb of Mary.[3]

Evidently even the Bible contains within itself the potential for
the destruction of this doctrine in any literal form. Furthermore,
it is almost certain on both literary and theological grounds, that
the birth narratives are later accretions to the original body of
gospel material. As Geza Vermes pertinently observes:

> The two principal properties of the infancy narratives, their
> anticipatory character in relation to the evolved message of
> Matthew and Luke and the fact that their peculiar feats are
> totally absent from the main body of the story of Jesus,
> demonstrate that they are later additions to the main gospel
> account.[4]

Moving on, then, from the problems inherent in the doctrine itself, there are also pressing reasons as to why it should forth-
with be dismantled, allowed to remain as a beautiful myth or
symbol testifying to the uniqueness of Jesus, but no longer at-
tached to what Küng so eloquently called an 'historical-biologi-
cal event'.

The principle reason for the argument for its demise as historical fact is that it is quite simply no longer necessary. It is redundant. We argued at length in Chapter Two that St
Augustine's doctrines of original sin and original guilt are thoroughly pernicious and need to be excised from all future

theological thinking, and logically once this is done there is no longer any necessity for a virginal conception of Jesus (nor for the Immaculate Conception of the Blessed Virgin Mary), since divinity no longer requires protection from contact with an ontologically tainted humanity. The way is clear for a normal human conception and birth and a christology of becoming such as has been outlined in Part One of this study.

As a corollary of this, we may also invoke the criterion of simplicity so beloved of those who work with mathematical theorems and scientific theories. The principle is that no theory should be more complicated than is necessary to explain whatever subject is under discussion, and that all unnecessary materials should be ruthlessly excluded, thus providing a theory that is as simple, and thereby as elegant, as possible. The same principle might usefully be employed in the realm of theology – which, after all, used to fancy itself as the 'queen of the sciences'. And according to this principle the result is exactly as outlined in the previous paragraph. The doctrine of the incarnation has for centuries been unnecessarily burdened with the doctrines of original sin, original guilt, virginal conception and (for Roman Catholics) Immaculate Conception. All are redundant, and without them the incarnation is revealed in the fullness of what might be called its 'simple wonder'.

Even more tellingly from the point of view of this study, the de-literalisation of the doctrine of the virginal conception of Jesus actually helps christology to make sense, and infinitely strengthens our picture of the union of the human and the divine in Jesus Christ. Indeed, although it may even sound shocking to those of a more traditional and conservative cast of mind, the doctrine of the virginal conception reduces the humanity of Jesus to a mere cipher and makes any truly satisfactory christology impossible – hence the metaphysical acrobatics performed by the early church fathers.

That this is so is so obvious that it is something of a wonder that it has not been remarked upon by everyone who has ever attempted christology. For if Jesus was virginally conceived then this, by definition, is a miracle planned and wrought by God. And this radically diminishes the humanity of Jesus, and not merely because it makes him the first human being to be deprived of a human father. Rather, it does so because it means, of necessity, that Jesus was to all intents and purposes pre-programmed to accomplish his task. There was no meaningful possibility that Jesus could at any point have said 'No' to God, or run away from his task or been anything but sinlessly perfect. Even for God, in these circumstances, the risk would be too great to be taken, for what would it mean if such a possibility of falling away was there and was actually realised? It would mean first and foremost that God had erred in performing his original miracle of virginal conception, and secondly that the Christ, the Son of God from the moment of his miraculous conception, was himself flawed. Such a scenario, even *in potentia*, is surely unthinkable, and therefore a virginally conceived Jesus must contain within himself no possibility of failure, which effectively reduces his humanity to little more than a chimera.

Conversely, a naturally conceived Jesus and a christology of becoming radically improves and renders more coherent our understanding of the incarnation. It relates humanity and divinity more intimately and more organically than any ontological and metaphysical approach, however subtly nuanced and highly organised, can ever do. Indeed, one of the major problems with such an approach is that however hard it tries to relate them, it is, in reality, always doomed to create a fundamental separation between God and humanity, creator and created, which itself renders the concept of incarnation almost impossible to understand or describe satisfactorily. This was recognised and strongly critiqued in her own day by Dorothy L. Sayers, but in all its essentials the situation has not changed a great deal in the intervening seventy years:

> Nor ... do the theologians of today take much trouble to expound their doctrine by way of the human maker's analogy ... the 'Creator-symbol' is used, if at all, to illustrate the deep gulf between God and his creatures.[5]

In direct contrast to such a gulf-centred theology, a christology of becoming spans the divide and places humanity and divinity in a position of profound interrelationship. In doing so it opens up new avenues of exploration in our relationship with Jesus and, as a direct consequence of this, also in our

understanding of what it means to be human and what the op-
portunities and capacities of humanity most truly are.

Specifically, a christology of becoming achieves four things,
all of which enrich our understanding both of incarnation and
of ourselves, which no more traditionally-based christology has
ever been able successfully to achieve. First, then, it allows for
(and indeed demands) the recognition of the absolute reality
and completeness of Jesus' human nature. In doing away with
St Augustine's version of original sin and original guilt and re-
moving the requirement for the virginal conception of Jesus,
such a christology ensures that Jesus is fully 'one of us'. This, I
suggest, is a deeply biblical insight which became progressively
obscured during the first few centuries of Christian history as
the person of Jesus of Nazareth became increasingly burdened
with the categories of classical metaphysics. The result has been
rather like a boat collecting barnacles: something of the original
shape may still be visible, but the object itself is entirely lost
from view under the accretions of time.

For the biblical writers themselves, however, the full humanity of Jesus was never in any doubt. Even Matthew and Luke,
who first (and almost certainly with primarily symbolic intent)
penned the stories of his virginal conception, never questioned
it and never jeopardised it by indulging in abstruse metaphysical speculation and thereby creating the insoluble 'oil and
water' problem of classical christology. The Jesus who strides
through the pages of the gospels is a fully rounded and dynamic
human being, and if anything puzzles his disciples it is not his
humanity but the apparent inbreaking of divinity into that humanity. In the gospels Jesus is a vibrant, compelling, challenging
and sometimes abrasive human being whose full humanity is
never open to question: it has been left to later generations to
water down that rich humanity into a set of metaphysical and
ontological formulae which do no justice to the stature of the
human character behind them. With the elegance of the novelist
and the acuity of the apologist, it is once again Dorothy L.
Sayers who pinpoints this transition at once deftly and savagely
in a passage deserving of extensive quotation:

So that is the outline of the official story – the tale of the time

when God was the under-dog and got beaten, when he sub-
mitted to the conditions He had laid down and became a
Man like the men He had made, and the men He had made
broke Him and killed Him. This is the dogma we find so dull
– this terrifying drama of which God is the victim and hero.

If this is dull, then what, in heaven's name, is worthy to be
called exciting? The people who hanged Christ never, to do
them justice, accused Him of being a bore – on the contrary;
they thought Him too dynamic to be safe. It has been left for
later generations to muffle up that shattering personality and
surround him with an atmosphere of tedium. We have very
efficiently pared the claws of the Lion of Judah, certified him
'meek and mild', and recommended Him as a fitting house-
hold pet for pale curates and pious old ladies. To those who
knew Him, however, He in no way suggested a milk-and-
water person; they objected to Him as a dangerous firebrand.
True, He was tender to the unfortunate, patient with honest
enquirers, and humble before Heaven; but He insulted respectable clergymen by calling them hypocrites; He referred
to King Herod as 'that fox'; He went to parties in disrep-
utable company and was looked on as a 'gluttonous man and
a wine-bibber, a friend of publicans and sinners'; He assault-
ed indignant tradesmen and threw them and their belong-
ings out of the Temple; He drove a coach-and-horses
through a number of sacrosanct and hoary regulations; He
cured diseases by any means that came handy, with a shocking casualness in the matter of other people's pigs and prop-
erty; He showed no proper deference for wealth and social
position; when confronted by neat dialectical traps, He dis-
played a paradoxical humour that affronted serious-minded
people, and He retorted by asking disagreeably searching
questions that could not be answered by rule of thumb. He
was emphatically not a dull man in His human lifetime, and
if He was God, there can be nothing dull about God either.[6]

But it is not only the gospels which demand that we respond
with full seriousness to the humanity of Jesus. One of the most
theologically sophisticated books of the New Testament, the
Epistle to the Hebrews, is eloquent on the subject:

> Therefore he had to become like his brothers and sisters in every respect, so that he might be a merciful and faithful high priest in the service of God, to make a sacrifice of atonement for the sins of the people. (2:17, *NRSV*)

> For we do not have a high priest who is unable to sympathise with our weaknesses, but we have one who in every respect has been tempted as we are, yet without sin. (4:15, *NRSV*)

In both gospels and epistles, then, the true and full humanity of Jesus is a fundamental given of faith, but it is one which – whatever lip-service may be paid to it – needs, theologically to be recovered from the God-heavy formulations of classical christology; and a christology of becoming begins, at least, in this regard from the right place, and enables us once more to see and rejoice in that complex and charismatic character, Jesus of Nazareth.

The second achievement of such a christology stems directly from this re-invigoration of the humanity of Jesus. And it is, quite simply, that we are enabled more clearly to recognise and rejoice in not just his 'oneness' with us, but also, logically and conversely, our 'oneness' with him. The relationship of being 'brothers' and 'sisters' with him, and therefore together children of God, becomes altogether more tangible and meaningful – and again these are insights which the biblical authors subscribed to unconditionally. In the context of traditional christology, though, it is hard (if not actually impossible) to feel oneself to be in a relation of brotherhood or sisterhood with a necessarily perfect Jesus who has been pre-ordained for Christ-ship. Once this system of patristic doctrinal accretion has been stripped away, however, the biblical conviction of this relationship can be allowed once again to speak with all its ancient power and authority. One might cite many passages, but nowhere does this voice speak with more power and rejoicing than in St Paul's Epistle to the Romans:

> For all who are led by the Spirit of God are children of God. For you did not receive a spirit of slavery to fall back into fear, but you have received a spirit of adoption. When we cry, 'Abba! Father!' it is that very Spirit bearing witness with

our spirit that we are children of God, and if children, then
heirs, heirs of God and joint heirs with Christ ... (8:14-17,
NRSV)

Here, indeed, is a joyous and passionate declaration of our
oneness with and in Jesus Christ.

A further corollary of this renewed (or, rather, re-found)
sense of oneness with Jesus is that the two great commandments
are bound indissolubly together through the person and work
of Jesus. Their content is familiar:

Hear what our Lord Jesus Christ says: You shall love the
Lord your God with all your heart and with all your soul and
with all your mind. This is the first and great commandment.
And the second is like it. You shall love your neighbour as
yourself.[7]

They are clearly intended to belong together and to form an organic unity ('The second is like it'), and I, personally, have always regarded them in this light. For many people, though, doctrine has forced them apart: one is a spiritual commandment
('Love God'), and one a material or fleshly commandment
('Love your neighbour'), and they apply within, as it were, different realms of being. Just how far apart they may be conceived
to be was brought forcibly home to me some thirty years ago
before I was even ordained. On a theological college parish
placement I had the temerity to preach on what I perceived as
the close relationship between the two great commandments,
and after the service I was brought up short by a peremptory
lecture from a somewhat crusty ex-military gentleman: 'Young
man,' he declaimed, 'There is a world of difference between loving God and loving your neighbour.' To be fair to him, from his
perspective, and from that of anybody brought up with traditional doctrinal formulations there probably is a world of difference (one heavenly, one earthly) between them; but from the
perspective of a christology such as we have described here the
two are firmly and inseparably yoked together, simply because
in loving Jesus Christ we already do both. Their original intended
unity (stressed by Jesus Christ himself) is reinforced in Jesus
Christ, rather than having the realms of human and divine firmly

delineated and demarcated as in so much of theological (and specifically christological) thinking down the ages. It is not merely biblical christology, but also many other aspects of biblical theology which are allowed to regain their true voice if we can step outside the limits which have previously been so rigidly imposed upon christological thinking.

The recovery of biblical theology may be significant, but the recovery of Jesus Christ himself is more significant still, and this represents the third achievement of a christology such as we have outlined here. We have already discussed the rediscovery of the vibrant humanity of Jesus, but here we are more concerned with the affective, emotional and spiritual impact of this newly rediscovered Jesus on the believer – although this is, of course, directly related to, and dependent upon, the prior re-affirmation of his full and dynamic humanity.

A question which we might do well to ask ourselves in this context is: 'Why did the disciples leave everything and follow Jesus, and why, wherever he went, were there always crowds of people jostling to be near him and listen to him?' The answer to this question must be simply that he was somebody who people wanted to be with and who spoke and acted so compellingly that they would not willingly miss one moment or one word. A parallel question which we might equally do well to ask ourselves is: 'Does this account resonate with the Jesus of my Sunday School, or Confirmation Classes, or average Sunday sermons?' And, sadly, the answer is almost certainly, 'No'. For the Jesus of Sunday School, Confirmation Class and sermon is the so-called 'Christ of faith' rather than the (notoriously hard to pin down) 'Jesus of history'; a Christ who comes pre-packaged in a kind of doctrinal cling-film:

> Furthermore it is necessary to everlasting salvation;
> that he also believe rightly the Incarnation of our Lord Jesus Christ.
> For the right Faith is that we believe and confess:
> that our Lord Jesus Christ, the Son of God, is God and Man:
> God, of the Substance of the Father, begotten before the worlds:
> and Man, of the Substance of his Mother, born in the world.

Perfect God, and perfect Man:
of a reasonable soul and human flesh subsisting:
equal to the Father, as touching his Godhead:
and inferior to the Father, as touching his Manhood.
Who although he be one God and Man, yet he is not two,
but one Christ:
One, not by conversion of the Godhead into flesh:
but by taking of the Manhood into God:
One altogether, not by confusion of Substance,
but by unity of Person.
For as the reasonable soul and flesh is one man:
so God and Man is one Christ.[8]

With this still re-printed in a supposedly 'contemporary' prayer book, is it any wonder that the church is a minority interest?

For there can be nothing especially attractive about a Jesus whose person and work (especially the atonement, of which more in the next chapter) are shrouded in some kind of metaphysical cat's-cradle. Even more so, there can be nothing spiritually or affectively compelling about a Jesus who had no choice but to be who he was, do what he did, and suffer what he suffered.

By contrast, a christology of becoming predicates a Jesus who constantly (though with periodic doubts, and on at least one occasion with the anguish of sweat like blood) chose to do what he did, suffer what he suffered, and thereby become who he was, and now forever, is. This is a compelling Jesus: a Jesus we might, as the disciples and crowds did, follow wherever he goes. This is a Jesus who does not inhabit our human flesh from above, but transforms it from within in perfect partnership with God; and this in turn leads seamlessly to the fourth achievement of a becoming christology which will be more fully explored in Chapter Eleven but which must be at least touched upon here in the context of our transformed appreciation of Jesus.

Thus, if what Jesus did was done – as we have argued it must have been – from a starting point in which he was genuinely and fully 'one of us', then what vistas of encouragement and inspiration this opens up for our own pilgrimage of *imitatio Christi*. We have touched on this theme in the context of 'One Christ or

Many Christs', but we may revisit it at least briefly here. Throughout its history Christianity has proclaimed the ideal of *imitatio Christi* with one hand, but with the other has withdrawn the possibility by stressing the innate depravity of humanity and the fact that we will be lucky to get into heaven at all! The doctrine of predestination (and especially Calvinistic double predestination) is a prime example of this. Taken literally it implies that no human striving for goodness counts in the heavenly scales: heaven or hell is pre-ordained no matter what we do. Humanity cannot even place its foot on the first rung of a heavenly ladder, and so, it might be asked, what purpose is there in aspiring to any sort of *imitatio Christi* in the first place?

I am not for one moment suggesting that we can earn our way into heaven, but merely that human nature needs its aspirations, and one of these, for those who seek to follow Jesus Christ is a genuine possibility of *imitatio*. To believe in this we need first to believe in the innate perfectibility of human nature (as we already believe happened in Jesus himself); not, in hubris, to believe necessarily that I will ever be perfect, but to believe that the nature of which I partake is, of its nature, capable of such perfection. An analogy might perhaps be of a child who starts to learn the violin. How depressing an experience this would be if it were known beforehand that even the best violinists never succeeded in making a noise which resembled anything other than a tortured cat! How much more will the child be inspired to strive if she has already heard recordings of the perfection of sound achieved by great violinists. The chance of actually emulating them may be small, but the desire and vision of the possibility will be there.

So too with our human nature. St Augustine's vision (and that of all who have followed him) of a human race naturally doomed to perdition is, spiritually speaking, thoroughly depressing, and however remote the chances of our attaining it we need, like the child learning the violin, both a vision of and a desire for the possibility of perfection. Such a vision of what our human nature might be is granted to us in the person of Jesus Christ as understood here, and from this vision a genuine desire for *imitatio Christi* may proceed.

Thus a Jesus restored to his full humanity impacts both upon our conception of Jesus himself and of ourselves. But a christo-logy of becoming re-vivifies not only the person of Jesus but also his work, and most especially the means through which, in him, our salvation has been wrought. We must therefore turn our at-tention next to the realm of soteriology, and specifically to the Doctrine of the Atonement.

Notes

1. Geza Vermes, *Jesus: Nativity – Passion – Resurrection*, London, Penguin Books, 2010, p 48.

2. Hans Küng, *On Being a Christian*, Latest edition London, Continuum, 2008, p 456.

3. James P. Mackey, *Jesus of Nazareth: The Life, the Faith and the Future of the Prophet (A Brief History)*, Dublin, The Columba Press, 2008, p 119.

4. Vermes, p 162.

5. Dorothy L. Sayers, *The Mind of the Maker*, London, Methuen, 1941, p 173.

6. Dorothy L. Sayers, *Creed or Chaos*, 'The Greatest Drama Ever Staged' in *Letters to a Diminished Church*, Nashville, Dallas, Mexico City, Rio de Janeiro & Beijing, Thomas Nelson, 2004, pp 1-7, pp 4-5 (First pub 1949).

7. As cited in, The General Synod of the Church of Ireland, *The Book of Common Prayer*, Dublin, The Columba Press, 2004, p 202.

8. As cited in, The General Synod of the Church of Ireland, *The Book of Common Prayer*, Dublin, The Columba Press, 2004, p 772.

CHAPTER TEN

Once for all upon the Cross

The realm of soteriology is a vast one, largely because in every age theologians have articulated a huge variety of different interpretations of the saving work of Christ. All, of course, reflect the fundamental belief that Christ has 'reconciled us to God in one body by the cross', but there is as almost infinite variation in the possibilities for deciding precisely who is saved and precisely how Jesus' death achieves that salvation. So enormous is the subject that when I was asked to teach a course on soteriology at the Church of Ireland Theological Institute I was allotted no fewer than twenty-one one hour lecture sessions – and as it turned out even this was not time to do more than scratch the surface of the subject.

So where do we begin? In that same lecture course I intro-duced the series of lectures with the following remarks, and they are equally germane here: 'We should begin by asking what the question or questions are that soteriology seeks to an-swer. And the questions are simple enough: it is only the plethora of possible answers which begins to get complicated. In essence the questions can be, effectively, reduced to one composite question: 'Who is saved, by whom, how, and from what?' Answer that and you are home and dry!'

For the purposes of the present discussion we are not con-cerned with the first or fourth parts of this question – with the niceties of exactly who is saved or what is the nature of that which they are saved from. Instead, our focus is solely on the second and third elements of the question: by whom are we saved and how (insofar as this can be articulated at all) does this salvation take place; and this leads us directly to the doctrine of the atonement.

As with all aspects of soteriology, the atonement is at once entirely simple and endlessly complicated: simple because every Christian would echo the basic phrase, 'Christ died for me'; but complicated because there is an almost endless variety of answers both to the exact nature of the person of Jesus Christ who died, and also to how that death achieved (and achieves) salvation and reconciliation with God.

One of the finest treatments of theories of the atonement in the last hundred years or so is that by the Swedish bishop and theologian, Gustaf Aulén, who wrote his celebrated treatise *Christus Victor* in 1930 and which was first published in English the following year. This book has had a major influence on all subsequent thinking on the atonement, and its stature within the theological world is readily attested to by the fact that eighty years later it is still in print. Aulén is so precise in his delineation of the various theories that it will be useful to consider his categorisation of them in more detail, as this will enable us to identify the flaw which is common to all of these traditional theories, and which can be avoided by means of a christology such as has been outlined in this volume.

Essentially, Aulén's achievement is to have identified and, in detail described, the three main types of atonement theory which have dominated all discussions of the subject. Clearly each of these has appeared in varying guises as they have been interpreted and adapted by individual theologians, but virtually all thinking on the atonement has been rooted in one of these three views. These views Aulén denominates as the 'Latin', the 'subjective' and the 'classic'.

The Latin view derives substantially from the thinking of St Anselm of Canterbury, and in particular from his book, *Cur Deus Homo?* In this work Anselm outlines a 'satisfaction' theory of the atonement, in which he 'put forward his teaching of a deliverance from the guilt of sin', and above all clearly taught an '"objective" Atonement, according to which God is the object of Christ's atoning work, and is reconciled through the satisfaction made to his justice.'[1] All subsequent manifestations of satisfaction theory find their roots in Anselm's exposition of it.

The 'subjective' view is one which has enjoyed a resurgence of popularity in recent generations, perhaps from as far back as the Enlightenment, probably as a result of a widespread dissatisfaction with the more extreme forms of the 'satisfaction' theory which had previously held sway. Its origins, though, are considerably more ancient than this, stemming, in large measure, from Peter Abelard. According to this theory the atonement consists 'essentially in a change taking place in men rather than a changed attitude on the part of God.'[2]

Since Anselm and Abelard, these two types of theory have been the dominant ones, but Aulén contends that there is a third theory which has for too long been ignored. It is, he says, the oldest theory of all, but was substantially eclipsed by Anselm and has never seriously reappeared since (although it should be noted that he also claims that Luther adhered more to it than to the Latin theory which he is usually assumed to have espoused). This third theory he calls the 'classic' theory, and he cites it as a 'dramatic' theory whose 'central theme is the idea of the Atonement as a Divine conflict and victory' in which:

> Christ – *Christus Victor* – fights against and triumphs over the evil powers of the world, the 'tyrants' under which mankind is in bondage and suffering, and in him God reconciles the world to himself.[3]

Having described the main characteristics of the three theories, Aulén then proceeds to compare them, and he does so in a manner which, from the standpoint of this discussion, perfectly highlights the fatal flaw which runs through all of them. Substantial quotation is necessary:

> The most marked difference between the 'dramatic' [classic] type and the so-called 'objective' [Latin] type lies is the fact that it [the classic type] represents the work of the Atonement as from first to last a work of God himself, a continuous Divine work; while according to the other view, the act of Atonement has indeed its origin in God's will, but is, in its carrying-out, an offering made to God by Christ as man and on man's behalf, and may therefore be called a discontinuous Divine work.
>
> On the other hand, it scarcely needs to be said that this 'dramatic' type stands in sharp contrast with the 'subjective' type of view. It does not set forth only or chiefly a change taking place in men; it describes a complete change in the

situation, a change in the relation between God and the world, and a change also in God's own attitude. The idea is, indeed, thoroughly 'objective'; and its objectivity is further emphasised by the fact that the Atonement is not regarded as affecting men primarily as individuals, but is set forth as a drama of the word's salvation.[4]

What Aulén is saying here is that the 'classic' theory is a work of God; the Latin theory is, in part at least, a work of man towards God; and the subjective theory is, to all intents and purposes, a work of man (though God-assisted) towards man.

Aulén, it seems to me, is right in saying this, but what he does not draw attention to – and nor, to my knowledge, has any-one else – is that each of these theories succeeds in setting up the same false dichotomy: that is, who acts towards whom? Is it God to God; God to man; man to God; or man to man?

The problem with the setting up of this dichotomy is that it reduces the salvific wonder of the atonement to a divine/human balancing act: can a human being do enough to satisfy God's sense of justice, or can God do enough to temper his own justice with mercy? How much does each party have to con-tribute before God and man can seal the bargain? Furthermore, it leaves the 'work' of man and the 'work' of God firmly placed in two separate compartments: even if Jesus himself is believed to be both human and divine, the various theories still stress the work of one of these natures above the other. Here, more plainly than anywhere else, the oil and water emulsion of Jesus' nature has begun disastrously to separate out.

In Part One of this study we have already argued that a christology of becoming engenders a far more organic unity of human and divine in Jesus than any more traditionally con-ceived christology is capable of doing, and both the truth of this and the importance of it are borne out if we apply the results of such a christology to the atonement.

For a becoming christology entirely does away with the need to balance the actions of God and humanity: there is no complex decision to be made as to who is acting upon whom. By the time of his trial and subsequent crucifixion, the person of Jesus of Nazareth has become the perfect meeting-place for God and

humanity, and in his own person his work becomes a quintes-
sential partnership between them, acting together to achieve
that reconciliation (and therefore salvation) for the human race
which God has always desired for it.

Indeed, with this perfect meeting point of divine and human
will in Jesus – which, of course, reached its fulfilment by the
time of Jesus' death and was later sealed and proclaimed by resurrection and ascension – it may be argued that there are here
the seeds of a richer and more fruitful picture of the atonement
than any of those to which we have grown so used over two
thousand years, and one which makes the work of atonement
the achievement of the whole life and death of Jesus rather than
merely of his death alone.

The concept of Jesus as the flawless meeting-place for divine
and human will is the key one here. This perfect alignment of
human and divine puts us in mind, by contrast, of their original
separation in the (mythical) sin of Adam. Many theologians
have remarked on this pairing of opposites, but among the original biblical writers it is St Paul who draws particular attention
to this:

> Therefore just as one man's trespass led to condemnation for
> all, so one man's act of righteousness leads to justification
> and life for all. For just as by the one man's disobedience the
> many were made sinners, so by the one man's obedience the
> many will be made righteous. (Romans 5:18-19, *NRSV*)

> For since death came by a human being, the resurrection of
> the dead has also come by a human being; for as all die in
> Adam, so all will be made alive in Christ. (1 Corinthians
> 15:21-22)

Apart from these overt references, there are many more places
where St Paul cites the 'obedience' of Jesus, and the use of such
vocabulary will always call to mind the original 'disobedience'
of Adam.

Perhaps, contra Aulén – and the rest of Christian history –
this is the oldest and most neglected atonement theory of them
all. Imprisoned by history and tradition we tend to think of
atonement in terms of sacrifice, of paying a price of some sort

and so on; but we should look again at the word 'atonement' – 'at-one-ment'. At the time of his death Jesus has become at one and the same time a human being and God; the two are 'at one' perfectly in him. Human and divine wills and natures meet once more and are perfectly reconciled in the person of Jesus Christ.

This possibility that the reconciliation of human and divine in the person of Jesus Christ is the dominant motif in the atonement (rather even than forgiveness of sins, since it may – and will – be argued that in this context reconciliation is prior to forgiveness) deserves closer attention, since if this possibility turns out to be justified, then we will need to learn to assimilate and live with a very different picture of atonement, but, I believe, a far richer one, than is any of those with which we have thus far been familiar.

Put bluntly, it is high time to launch an attack on all traditional theories of the atonement, for in the various forms in which we have inherited it, it is as beset with problems as the Graeco-Latin metaphysical speculations as to the nature of Jesus which prompted this book in the first place; and a Jesus who becomes the Christ hints at a revised estimate of the atonement in keeping with this new vision of Jesus himself.

It may sound shocking to some (though perhaps balm to others), but Christianity has always had a compulsive obsession with sin, guilt, forgiveness and sacrifice, and these have therefore become key concepts in interpreting the salvific death of Jesus Christ. After two millennia the formula simply trips off the tongue:

> It [the Christian story] recounts the sacrifice, the self-immolation of the Son of God who willingly offered his life, we are told, for the redemption of the sins of mankind.[5]

Admittedly it is not difficult to see where the dependence on these categories of thought came from. Christianity had (and has) its roots firmly in Judaism, and all of the apostles and the earliest writers on this new faith would have been (like Jesus himself, of course) Jews.

It would therefore have been natural for them to have cast the New Covenant in the outward form of the Old, a process taken to the highest degree by the author of the Epistle to the

Hebrews, who envisages the relationship between the two covenants almost Platonically, the Old being an inferior version of the New Covenant which stands as a 'form'. For all of the New Testament writers, though, the Old Covenant was firmly present in their thinking. This Mosaic Covenant was based on law – indeed on thousands of laws covering all the possible business of life. Laws, by definition, can be broken, thus incurring sin and guilt. Sin requires forgiveness, and as in almost all ancient cultures the route to forgiveness is sacrifice, and hence the Covenant is underpinned by regulations for sin and guilt offerings to expiate the sins of the people. It is perhaps, hardly surprising, therefore, that sin, guilt, forgiveness and sacrifice came so quickly to be such influential concepts in the newly-emerging faith of Christianity, and rapidly came to govern the imagery and reasoning behind the death of Jesus Christ.

But it may cogently be argued – and it is at once refreshing and alarming to be questioning two thousand years of tradition – that this insistence on these things as the predominant categories by which to understand Jesus' death was, in fact, a very long-lasting false start, and that we need radically to re-envision just what it is that Jesus' death achieves.

We will consider the New Covenant presently, but it is important to note that even under the Old Covenant there were periodic prophetic voices raised as to the adequacy, or otherwise, of a faith based on sin and sacrifice. In particular it is the three (arguably) greatest of the so-called Minor Prophets, Hosea, Amos and Micah, who question whether sacrifice is an adequate – or even appropriate – medium for the conduct of a religion. For them, other values such as justice and mercy are far more important and no amount of sacrifice can ever atone for the absence of these prior concepts. Consider, for example, the following passages:

> For I desire steadfast love and not sacrifice, the knowledge of God rather then burnt offerings. (Hosea 6:6, *NRSV*)

> Though they offer choice sacrifices, though they eat flesh, the Lord does not accept them. (Hosea 8:13, *NRSV*)

> They shall not pour drink-offerings of wine to the Lord, and

their sacrifices shall not please him. Such sacrifices shall be like mourners' bread; all who eat of it shall be defiled; for their bread shall be for their hunger only; it shall not come to the house of the Lord. (Hosea 9:4, *NRSV*)

I hate, I despise your festivals, and I take no delight in your solemn assemblies. Even though you offer me your burnt-offerings and grain-offerings, I will not accept them; and the offerings of well-being of your fatted animals I will not look upon. Take away from me the noise of your songs: I will not listen to the melody of your harps. But let justice roll down like waters, and righteousness like an ever-flowing stream. (Amos 5:21-24, *NRSV*)

He has told you, O mortal, what is good: and what does the Lord require of you but to do justice and love kindness, and to walk humbly with your God? (Micah 6:8, *NRSV*)

For these prophets, at least, the place of sacrifice at the heart of faith is not unchallengeable or self-evident. Sacrifice does not atone for sins which are un-repented and on-going, and repent-ance – meaning, as it does, not a wallowing in remorse, but a change of direction, and as expressed in doing justice, loving kindness and walking humbly with God – obviates the need (if there ever was one) for sacrifice anyway.

This sense of an inward turning being of vastly more signific-ance than any outward act such as sacrifice is also reflected in the major prophets, especially in Jeremiah and Ezekiel, both of whom use the image of Israel being given a new heart and a new spirit – a gift which does not depend upon sacrifice but solely upon the gracious will of God to draw near to his people and to enable them, through grace, to draw near once more to him.

When we turn to the New Covenant in Jesus Christ we should immediately notice two central – but almost universally overlooked – features. First, and perhaps surprisingly, given just how deeply ingrained the phraseology has become in the Christian psyche through its daily repetition in the liturgy of the church, there is the paucity of references, especially in the gospels, to any idea that Christ died 'for our sins'. The relevant passages from the institution narratives (and I include St Paul's version from 1 Corinthians) are:

While they were eating, Jesus took a loaf of bread, and after blessing it he broke it, gave it to the disciples, and said, 'Take, eat; this is my body.' Then he took a cup, and after giving thanks he gave it to them, saying, 'Drink from it all of you; for this is my blood of the covenant, which is poured out for many for the forgiveness of sins.' (Matthew 26:26-28, *NRSV*)

While they were eating, he took a loaf of bread, and after blessing it he broke it, gave it to them, and said, 'Take; this is my body.' Then he took a cup, and after giving thanks he gave it to them, and all of them drank from it. He said to them, 'This is my blood of the covenant, which is poured out for many.' (Mark 14:22-24, *NRSV*)

Then he took a loaf of bread, and when he had given thanks, he broke it and gave it to them, saying, 'This is my body, which is given for you. Do this in remembrance of me.' And he did the same with the cup after supper, saying, 'This cup that is poured out for you is the new covenant in my blood.' (Luke 22:19-20, *NRSV*)

... the Lord Jesus on the night when he was betrayed took a loaf of bread, and when he had given thanks, he broke it and said, 'This is my body that is for you. Do this in remembrance of me.' In the same way he took the cup also, after supper saying, 'This cup is the new covenant in my blood. Do this, as often as you drink it, in remembrance of me.' (1 Corinthians 11:23-25, *NRSV*)

Of the four versions given, only Matthew's goes so far as to say 'for the forgiveness of sins'. Of the four accounts, St Paul's is certainly the oldest, and St Mark's is almost certainly the first of the gospel accounts. St Matthew has therefore added to a pre-existing tradition which did not spell out Jesus' death as being 'for the forgiveness of sins', but was content to assert that it was simply 'for us' – which, of course, allows for a far wider range of interpretation.

Moreover, it can cogently be argued that Matthew is not implying – as phrases such as this are so often interpreted as meaning – that Jesus died *in order* that sins might be forgiven. It is equally, if not more likely, that Matthew is saying that through his death Jesus reveals how sins may be forgiven (that is, by refusing to retaliate or bear ill-will no matter how great the sin), and therefore dies in order that his followers may imitate his example of forgiveness, which is itself the New Covenant – replacing the Old Covenant with its emphasis on sacrifice. In support of such a concept, Edward Schweizer, one of the foremost New Testament scholars of the twentieth century, has this to say:

> The added phrase 'for the forgiveness of sins' was omitted by Matthew in his account of John's baptism …; in the story of the paralytic, however, he speaks not only of Jesus' authority to forgive sins, but also that of the community … Matthew thus looks upon the death of Jesus as the basis for the forgiveness of sins, albeit in such a way that forgiveness is exercised by the community … and that only the man who forgives others can receive forgiveness …
>
> Matthew thus probably sees Jesus going to his death less as an atoning sacrifice to God's obduracy … than as a pioneer, who opens the way of a new life to those who follow him …[6]

Apart from the institution narratives, Jesus speaks of his death on a variety of occasions, such as the celebrated three predictions of his death in St Mark's gospel (and parallels), but on none of these occasions does he say anything about his death being for the 'forgiveness of sins'. The only occasion on which there is any suspicion of such an interpretation is when in St Mark's gospel James and John (or in Matthew, their mother) spark off a discussion concerning greatness among the disciples. Jesus rebukes them and concludes by teaching about servanthood. The relevant passages are:

> For the Son of Man came not to be served but to serve, and to give his life as a ransom for many. (Mark 10:45, *NRSV*)

> … just as the Son of Man came not to be served but to serve, and to give his life a ransom for many. (Matthew 20:28, *NRSV*)

> For who is greater, the one who is at the table or the one who serves? Is it not the one at the table? But I am among you as one who serves. (Luke 22:27, *NRSV*)

Of the three passages it is St Luke's version, without the image of ransom (and in which the image of service is most appropriate, being actually set in the context of a meal) which appears to be the most authentic one in terms of actually reflecting the words of Jesus himself. Again it is Schweizer, commenting this time on St Mark's version which St Matthew simply adopts virtually unchanged, who clarifies the situation: '... vs. 45 is an explanation which has been added by the church ... vs. 45 did not originate with Jesus but with the Jewish-Christian church.'[7] Within the gospels, then, there is little or nothing to suggest that Jesus himself viewed his death as being primarily (or even at all) associated with the forgiveness of sins, and certainly nothing in connection with the all-too-common understanding that this death had to happen before sins could be forgiven, an idea which appears to be totally foreign to the biblical accounts.

Even if we leave the gospels to one side and turn to the more apparently fruitful figure of St Paul, there are, perhaps surprisingly, in the seven letters of which he is definitely the author, very few explicit references in which Paul interprets Jesus' death in terms of forgiveness. The passages where such a view is put forward are: Romans 3:21-26, 4:25 and 8:3-4, 1 Corinthians 5:7 and 15:3, and Galatians 1:4. Interestingly, there are at least three other passages which are often interpreted in this light, but which are, in fact, saying something subtly but vitally different. These passages are: 2 Corinthians 5:14-21, Romans 5:19, and Romans 5:6-11, which, being the most extensive and important, is deserving of quotation:

> For while we were still weak, at the right time Christ died for the ungodly. Indeed, rarely will anyone die for a righteous person – though perhaps for a good person someone might actually dare to die. But God proves his love for us in that while we were still sinners Christ died for us. Much more surely then, now that we have been justified by his blood, will we be saved through him from the wrath of God. For if while we were enemies, we were reconciled to God through the death of his Son, much more surely having been reconciled will we be saved by his life. But more than that, we even boast in God through our Lord Jesus Christ, through whom we have now received reconciliation. (*NRSV*)

Certainly this passage refers to us as ungodly, as sinners and as enemies, and speaks of our justification by Christ's blood, but it nowhere links these things irrevocably and necessarily with the forgiveness of sins, nor, even more particularly with the ability or willingness of God to forgive them. Indeed, it may well be argued that another motif altogether is the dominant one here, and that is the theme of reconciliation; and the same would to all intents and purposes be true if we were to analyse the other two passages mentioned above. And the reconciliation of humanity with God is, as we have seen, precisely what is achieved perfectly in Jesus Christ according to a christology of becoming. Again it seems as though the idea might not be so unbiblical after all.

We are left, admittedly, with the irreducible half-a-dozen or so occasions on which St Paul does interpret Jesus' death directly in terms of the forgiveness of sins, but it is hardly surprising, given his background, that he should have done so at least some of the time. Prior to his conversion on the Road to Damascus he had been an archetypical (and ultra-zealous) Jew, and all his life he would have lived in an atmosphere of sacrifice and atonement for sins: is it any wonder that at least some of the time he applied these same categories of thought to the death of Jesus? What is perhaps more surprising, and therefore more noteworthy, is that he did not do so all the time, and that other categories of interpretation such as reconciliation also play such a major part in his thinking. Furthermore, the fact that St Paul thought at least in part of an atoning sacrifice is no binding reason why we should have to do so, given that we do not share St Paul's background and culture, and that Jesus himself appears not to have thought in this way. We may, and should, feel free to develop potentially more creative and powerful interpretations of his death, and ones which are more organically linked with the whole of the rest of his life.

The second thing to notice about the New Covenant is that it is the consistent teaching of Jesus that forgiveness does not depend upon sacrifice or death. Forgiveness of sins is freely available to all – subject, as we shall see, to only one overriding condition. It would be possible to trawl through all four gospels and cite a plethora of examples (especially as Matthew, Mark and Luke very frequently have parallel accounts of the same incident), and so in order to avoid death by exegetical tedium, I have selected almost at random a few pertinent examples. In Matthew 9 (vv 2-8) there is the story of the paralysed man lowered through the roof whose sins Jesus forgives; Matthew 18:21-33 contains the parable of the forgiven debtor who is only 'unforgiven' when he himself refuses to forgive; and St Luke's gospel offers us the parable of the prodigal son (15:11-32) who is not merely forgiven but rejoiced over by his father, and also the memorable story of Zacchaeus of whom, after he has promised to repay anyone whom he has defrauded, Jesus said, 'Truly, salvation has come to this house'.

Most telling of all, though, is Matthew 6:12-15, which sets out the fundamental principle of the reciprocity of forgiveness, the one condition mentioned above: if we forgive, we will be forgiven; if we do not forgive, we will not be forgiven. This passage is so significant as to demand quotation:

> And forgive us our debts, as we also have forgiven our debtors. And do not bring us to the time of trial, but rescue us from the evil one. For if you forgive others their trespasses, your heavenly Father will also forgive you; but if you do not forgive others, neither will your Father forgive your trespasses. (*NRSV*)

What is striking about this passage is the emphasis which Jesus places on forgiving in order to be forgiven. The same idea appears, of course, as we noted above, in the parable of the forgiven debtor, but here it is spelt out unmistakeably as Jesus provides a gloss on the last but one petition of Matthew's version of the Lord's Prayer. What is made devastatingly obvious is that our forgiveness depends not upon death or sacrifice, but on our forgiveness of others. Those who forgive are, or will be, forgiven.

The picture that emerges from this survey of the biblical material is one that is very different from the dominant traditional viewpoint that Jesus Christ died 'for the forgiveness of our sins' – this interpretation being a later accretion to the initial governing metaphor of reconciliation as being the principal achievement of Jesus' death, as indeed it was of his whole life, a fact which a christology of becoming is at pains to emphasise.

What was most significant about the death of Jesus,

then – and this is entirely in keeping with a christology of becoming – is not that it was in any way a propitiation of God or a
penal substitution, but that it was precisely the result of Jesus'
never-ending lifelong 'Yes' to God through teachings, healings,
controversies and so on, and from which he steadfastly refused
to swerve even when it led to direct confrontation, arrest, trial
and death. Through this process human and divine wills are perfectly united and therefore reconciled in the person of Jesus, and
we are therefore, as sharing in that same human nature, perfectly reconciled to God in him. Most certainly Jesus died 'for us'
and 'once for all' upon the cross, but a christology of becoming
sees this in an altogether more positive and creative light than a
more traditional presentation with its less than helpful and
more or less exclusive emphasis on the paired concepts of sin
and sacrifice derived from the Old Covenant.

Notes
1. Gustav Aulén, *Christus Victor*, trs A. G. Hebert, London, SPCK, 2010,
p 2.
2. Ibid.
3. Ibid., p 4.
4. Ibid., pp 5-6.
5. Geza Vermes, *Jesus: Nativity – Passion – Resurrection*, London, Penguin
Books, 2010, p 169.
6. Eduard Schweizer, *The Good News According to Matthew*, London,
SPCK, 1976, (Fourth Impression, 1982), p 491.
7. Eduard Schweizer, *The Good News According to Mark*, London, SPCK,
1971, (Sixth Impression, 1981), p 219.

CHAPTER ELEVEN

Receiving the Christ

In the course of the previous two chapters we have explored some essential features both of the person and of the work of Jesus Christ. As a corollary of this, it is now important to illustrate the significance of a christology of becoming for our own experience of Jesus and our recognition of him as the Christ. In doing this we will discover that a becoming christology better illuminates and enhances the meaningfulness of Jesus as the Christ.

For the problem with the picture of Jesus as traditionally conceived and metaphysically clothed is that he just ontologically *is* the Christ. As soon as Jesus was born in Bethlehem, then also, as the Christmas carol puts it, 'Christ was born in Bethlehem'. Clearly, though, from the perspective of this study, we would wish to argue that although this turned out to be so, it was not necessarily the case.

Undoubtedly the position that Jesus just is the Christ is a very comfortable position to adopt, since it leaves aside the uncomfortable possibility that the incarnation might have failed; but for all its reassuring certainty it is also an entirely static and ultimately sterile vision of Jesus and his Christ-ship.

It is so because from within this perspective it does not logically matter – although it may of course matter a great deal to any given individual, but this is a different issue – whether anyone ever recognised – or recognises – the nature of Jesus as being the Christ. Whether people recognise him or not, this simply is what he is. In theory, at least, it would be possible to have an incarnation which went entirely unnoticed, and this would make no difference to the fact of the incarnation. God would still have walked this earth in human form, even if no-one had actually spotted him.

For a christology of becoming, however, this simply will not do. And it will not do for at least three reasons. First, the nature of the Christ must be recognised in order to be meaningful: Jesus' Christ-ship was not an ontological given which depended upon nothing else for its reality. Rather, his becoming the Christ was dependent at least in part on others recognising and receiving him as such, and thereby giving him the courage of his own slowly developing conviction that this might indeed be his vocation. We have previously examined several episodes of becoming, and have seen that particularly in his question to the disciples, 'But you, who do you say that I am?' there is a burning need for recognition and thereby reassurance within the person of Jesus himself.

For a Jesus who simply was the Christ, there is no possible need for such a question – other, perhaps, than simply as a piece of stage-management to elicit the appropriate confessional response from Peter. By contrast, for a Jesus who is in process of becoming the Christ, the question is a real and urgent one, demanding not a set-piece confession but a genuine answer upon which much of Jesus' future ability to continue his path of becoming will depend.

The teachings, preachings and healings of Jesus are not a form of divine *quod errat demonstrandum* appended to the final page of Jesus' divine CV; rather they are a continual working-out of his divine vocation, and subject always both to the human Jesus' ongoing 'Yes' to God, and to his capacity to believe in his own vocation and to communicate that vocation to his hearers – and, indeed, to articulate it in dialogue with them. If it is to be truly meaningful, the Christ-ship of Jesus depends as much upon its recognition by his disciples as it does upon its dawning reality within his own psyche. And the same equation holds good for future generations of believers. The fact that we now recognise Jesus as the Christ depends principally upon the witness of that first generation with whom he interrelated, and to whom he manifested himself progressively during his life, and ultimately, as St Paul attests, by resurrection, as the Christ. If that identity had not been forged and recognised, then later generations would have, quite literally, nothing to go on; and even more tellingly, if his potential identity as the Christ had not been recognised 'in the making' as it were, then there is a very real question as to whether it would ever have reached fruition.

Let us imagine, for a moment, a different version of Jesus' interrogation of the disciples in Mark 8 which we examined in Chapter Four.

> ... on the way he asked his disciples, 'Who do people say that I am?' And they answered him, 'John the Baptist, and others Elijah, and still others one of the prophets.' He asked them, 'But who do you say that I am?' Peter answered him, 'Truly we have no idea.'

Could Jesus' emerging self-identity have survived such a scenario? On the whole, I rather think not.

As we have already observed, a Jesus who was necessarily the Christ would not depend upon recognition – he just would be the Christ whether or not anyone recognised him. But how much more compelling, dynamic and magnetic is a Christ of becoming. Such a Christ relates to the crowds and to his disciples in a shared, reciprocal process of recognition and becoming. And once again this is a reflection of God's way of partnership with humanity: the full realisation of Jesus' Christ-ship depends not solely upon him (although obviously his ceaseless 'Yes' is the primary criterion), but also upon the response of those whom Jesus meets, teaches, heals and so on.

Secondly, however, it was not merely that Jesus' emerging self-identity had to be forged in the context of his preaching, teaching and healing and in his contact with all those whom he met; but it is also vital to the integrity (and to the wonder and mystery) of our salvation, that this identity should have been fashioned in the midst of the real world of human sin, greed, cruelty, egoism and the like. That this must be so may be simply illustrated. There is an old philosophical/theological conundrum which begins by lamenting the fallenness and evil of the world, and specifically the reality that human beings, when faced with moral choices between good and evil, right and wrong, so often choose the evil and the wrong. Would it not have been better, it is then suggested, if God had created a world in which there was no possibility of evil or wrongdoing, and where only the good could possibly be chosen? But, the conundrum asks finally, in a world where there is no evil and no possibility of evil, what possible meaning has the concept of goodness? Does not the concept of goodness itself cease to exist in such a world; and does not the existence of goodness depend, in the end, upon the existence of its opposite? Ergo, in fact, God has created the only sort of world in which goodness can possibly have any meaning or moral value.

In essence this conundrum applies precisely to the nature of Jesus. As traditionally conceived and presented he is – in spite of the (according to this traditional understanding) token gesture of the temptation narratives – incapable of sin, and this rather vitiates the value of his perfection in the midst of the real, everyday world of mingled sin and goodness. It is a perfection which could not have been other than it was, and which therefore largely fails to speak to the rest of the (imperfect) human race. This Jesus appears as an alien construct dropped ready-made from another world. It is Messiah-ship 'Blue Peter' style: 'I have one here I prepared earlier.' The poet Stevie Smith, who was also a highly competent theologian and a frequent reviewer of theological books, expresses this insight particularly astutely, and with it her – and many other people's frustration with Christianity:

> Oh Christianity, Christianity,
> Why do you not answer our difficulties?
> If He was God He was not like us,
> He could not lose.[1]

For the Christ-ship and perfection of Jesus to be existentially real and meaningful, they have to have been forged in the same world which the rest of humanity inhabits and therefore recognises, and not in some far-off celestial workshop.

Thus far, then, we have argued first that Jesus' Christ-ship was at least in part dependent upon the recognition of him by others – and especially by his closest circle of followers – and secondly that his Christ-ship needed to be worked out in the same world as that in which those followers lived. First, Christ is recognised as such (however falteringly) by others; secondly, he inhabits their world.

Thirdly then, these insights then coalesce and are reflected in a christology of becoming in Jesus' own recognition of the state of that world: as his followers recognise his condition (of becoming), so he recognises their condition (of fallenness) and the need for action (both divine, and, responsively, human) to address and rectify it. It is, as we have noted previously, St Paul who creatively develops the First Adam / Last Adam typology to characterise Jesus' work of reconciliation. Jesus himself makes no such comparison, and yet there are clear indications that Jesus was convinced of the need for perfect human obedience to, and cooperation with God if humanity was, through a human life, to be reconciled with God. He knew, it seems, the need for that reconciliation and redemption to be realised and incarnated in one human being in order for it to be made real for all humanity.

This obedience, co-operation and concomitant oneness with God are primary themes both of Jesus' speech and action. Admittedly the different gospel writers stress different things and express them in different conceptual language, but the underlying reality is the same. In St John's gospel the governing metaphor is 'oneness', especially in Jesus' great final discourse and subsequent prayer at the Last Supper. The initial oneness is that which exists between Jesus and the Father: 'Believe me that I am in the Father and the Father is in me ...' (14:11), and this is to be reflected both among his followers and between those followers and Jesus and the Father: 'As you, Father, are in me and I am in you, may they also be in us, so that the world may believe that you have sent me. The glory that you have given me I have given them, so that they may be one as we are one, I in them and you in me, that they may become completely one ...' (17:21b-23a). Through Jesus' perfect obedience, co-operation and consequent oneness with the Father comes about, reconciliation and subsequent oneness for the rest of humanity, both on a horizontal human-human, and vertical human-divine plane.

The synoptic gospels do not speak the same poetic and quasi-mystical language of oneness as John, but the underlying theme of obedience and co-operation recognised and exemplified in and by Jesus is equally clear nonetheless.

Perhaps the most significant witness to this in the preaching of Jesus in the synoptic gospels is the number of parables which deal with the relationship of servant to master, highlighting the need for obedience to the master's will, and with these, the revealing story of the two sons, one who says 'Yes' and does not act, and the other who initially says 'No', but later obeys (Matthew 21:28-31).

Standing far over and above all this teaching – and, of course, eternally validating it – is the witness to obedience and co-oper-ation of Jesus' life itself. It is all very well to preach obedience; it is quite another to live it, to live it at personal cost, and to live it as compellingly as Jesus does. We may see this obedience in the (admittedly stylised) temptation stories; we may see it in the re-solve with which Jesus refuses to be browbeaten or warned off by the increasingly hostile religious establishment; and we may see it above all in the Garden of Gethsemane.

We have already visited this episode once in the context of the contingency of Jesus' Christ-ship (he could have walked away and failed to become the Christ); but here we must explore this passage from the perspective of Jesus' own growing sense of identity and commitment to obedience and co-operation (his 'Yes' to God) if he was to fulfil his unique vocation to Christ-ship.

And it is here in the Garden that we see most compellingly of all Jesus' nascent Christ-ship and his full humanity, stretched here to its utmost limits in its passionate, agonised quest for obedience and co-operation, and through them for the final stages of divine becoming. For let us make no mistake about it, Jesus did not want to be in that garden and, as we have already seen, he did not have to be there: he could simply have slipped quietly away.

Being there was itself agony, an agony which must have been doubled and re-doubled by the knowledge of the inevitability of what was to come if he remained there. The gospels themselves make this very plain. Mark's Jesus is 'distressed and agitated' and 'deeply grieved, even to death' (14:33-34). Matthew simply follows this pattern, but Luke is even more graphic: 'In his an-guish he prayed more earnestly, and his sweat became like great drops of blood falling down on the ground' (22:44).

The trembling, fearful humanity of Jesus would rather be anywhere else than here. Yet by this stage in his career the union between Jesus of Nazareth and the Christ is so complete that even as he prays agitatedly, 'Take this cup from me', he can also add, 'Yet not what I want, but what you want.' Here, in perfect obedience, the disobedience of the First Adam is annulled once and for all, and all are reconciled to God in Christ.

In this sense – of recognising the need for both obedience to God and identification with fallen humanity – Jesus' career comes full circle: as T. S. Eliot put it, 'In my end is my beginning'. For Jesus' public ministry was inaugurated by his baptism at the hands of John the Baptist. This baptism was unnecessary from the point of view of the forgiveness of sins – and indeed Matthew's gospel portrays John as remonstrating with Jesus and arguing that Jesus should be baptising him. Yet Jesus is baptised, not for the forgiveness of sins, but as a sign and seal of obedience ('This is/you are my son, with whom I am well-pleased'), and as a pledge of oneness with sinful humanity also.

In a variety of ways, then, in this chapter we have traced at least briefly a number of the means by which a christology of becoming is enriched and enhanced by the mutual processes of Jesus' own recognition of his divine vocation as the Christ, and other people's dawning perception of him as such.

What emerges from this process is a rounded and compelling Christ who was then, and is now, in a deep reciprocal relationship – of recognition, showing forth and discovery – with his people. This Christ – rather than the traditional ready-made, pre-packaged Christ – is a Christ who has the depth and charisma to utter those words of calling to us as he did to the first disciples: 'Follow me'. How a Christ of becoming impinges creatively upon our following we must now, therefore, explore.

Notes
1. Stevie Smith, 'Oh Christianity, Christianity', *The Collected Poems of Stevie Smith*, Harmondsworth, Penguin, 1985, p 416.

CHAPTER TWELVE

A Covenant People

The concept of covenant is central to the thinking of the Bible in both the Old and the New Testaments. Indeed, these divisions of the Bible are also known as (but not as frequently referred to as) the Old and New Covenants. 'Covenant' is also a word which has come to occupy theological and ecclesiological centre-stage at the present time through the presence of such things as the recent Anglican Covenant as an attempt to repair the current divisions within that communion, and the proposed Anglican-Methodist covenant. It is therefore worth exploring this concept in some detail, in order to see whether, and if so how, a christology of becoming might shed new light on, and enrich the relationships enshrined in the New Covenant in particular.

We must begin with the Old Testament (Covenant), however, since it is here that the idea of covenant was, religiously speaking, within the Judeo-Christian tradition at least, first established. With regard to the concept of covenant in the Old Testament there has been speculation that it may have been based on agreements common in the ancient middle east between conquering nations and their vassal states. For the purposes of the present discussion, whether this is correct or not is of little moment, although I would argue that even if it is correct, the idea had undergone substantial change before it reached the Old Testament, where covenants are tinged with love, rather than the suppression of an underlying hatred.

The governing Old Testament covenant is, of course, the covenant of Sinai, enshrined in the giving of the Ten Commandments, and thereafter fleshed out in the entirety of the Torah – the Law – which was to be Israel's response of obedience to God's gracious promises. For the Jewish people this was, and is, the definitive covenant, for it is what defined them as a people, even though, as yet, they had no homeland, and formulated and

cemented their unique relationship with God as his chosen people.

It was, however, neither the first nor the last covenant in the
Old Testament. Prior to this God had made covenants with
Noah and with Abraham. To Noah he had given the sign of the
rainbow as a promise that he would never again inundate the
earth, and to Abraham he gave the promise – unlikely though it
undoubtedly seemed to Abraham and Sarah – that his descend-
ants would be as numberless as the grains of sand or the stars in
the sky. Also, in addition to these previous covenants, God later
made a covenant with David, promising that if David and his
successors remained faithful to God then there would always be
a descendant of David on the throne of Israel.

For all of these different circumstances, though, there is an
underlying unity of structure running through these various
covenants to which we must pay close attention, in order to see
in due course how this pattern is taken up and at once fulfilled
and transformed in a New Covenant based on a christology of
becoming.

In essence, then, there are at least three distinguishing features of all of these Old Testament covenants. The first such feature is that there is a stated and overt obligation on both sides,
confirmed, usually, by specific promises. A covenant is not a
vague agreement to keep the peace or to be unspecifically forgiving, nice or generous to one another. Rather, it is a legally
framed agreement incorporating very particular clauses and
pledges. Typically, the form of covenant in the Old Testament
consists of promises of blessing from God and reciprocal
promises of obedience and faithfulness from his people. That
this should be so is hardly surprising; indeed any other format is
almost unthinkable. God cannot be required to promise faithfulness (to be anything other than faithful would be contrary to his
nature), and his people cannot promise blessings, but only
obedience. Thus, as we have seen, God promises, variously, no
more floods, descendants, a Promised Land and successors on
the throne of Israel: conversely, the people of the covenant
promise simple fidelity in order to receive these promised blessings.

The second notable aspect of a covenant relationship is that there are penalties for reneging on the covenant. Here, it is true, there may well be echoes of the secular and political peace-keep-ing covenant. But even here the terms of the covenant are soft-ened when it comes to the relationship between God and his people. In secular terms, a conquering ruler could impose, effect-ively, whatever conditions he chose upon his vassal states. Reneging on a covenant might mean the death of a puppet king and courtiers, renewed exile, the sack of a city or whatever.

God, however, is primarily merciful rather than vengeful. The breaking of a covenant by the covenant people will tend to mean the withdrawal of blessings rather than wholesale de-struction. Thus the people of Israel wandered for forty years in the wilderness until all of the faithless generation who baulked at the spies' report had perished; and Israel lost its united king-dom and both the northern and southern kingdoms suffered de-feat and exile as a result of the faithlessness of David's descend-ants. If the concept of covenant did derive from ancient Middle-Eastern peace agreements, then here is at least some softening of the original framework, and we shall see in due course how much the framework is again restructured and made altogether more tender through a christology of becoming.

The third distinguishing feature of the Old Testament con-cept of covenant represents an even greater departure from its military and political origins, and forms a pointer to what will become evident in the New Testament if a christology of becom-ing is espoused. This is the simple fact that all of the covenants (Noah, Abraham, Moses and David) which we have touched on so far go (if not explicitly, at least implicitly) a great deal further than merely promises, obligations and penalties. Each of them, whatever the terms, obligations or penalties spelled out, implies a passionate and genuinely reciprocal relationship of trust, faithfulness and, ultimately, love, which goes far deeper than any wish simply to 'keep the peace' or keep a subject people in check. Covenant in the Old Testament is not about mere subject-ion: it is about God leading his people towards loving obedience and faithfulness to his will, which is, and always has been, set solely and passionately towards their good; indeed, their salva-tion, as we shall see in the New Testament.

We are led inexorably, therefore, to the subject of the New

Covenant as outlined in the New Testament, and to the possibilities for such a covenant as conceived by a traditional christology – whether from above or below, whether based on a difference of degree or kind – or alternatively through a christology of becoming.

In earlier chapters we have explored already some of the shortcomings of all traditional christological methods, and in particular the problem of how all such methods cannot do other – however unintentionally, and however much window-dressing there may be to try to mask the fact – than significantly to downplay the importance of Jesus' human nature. Humanity becomes swamped by divinity, until it is hard to conceive of Jesus being 'like us' in any genuinely meaningful sense.

Flowing from this is one of the most serious objections which may be levelled at this kind of christology: namely, that it fails to provide – in spite of the fact that it most certainly claims to do so – a truly new and radical re-interpretation of our covenant relationship with God.

The problem stems from the fact that without exception, all traditional christologies presuppose – even if the presupposition is never overtly voiced – that Jesus was necessarily the Christ: he could not have been otherwise. If this presupposition is correct, and Jesus of Nazareth was necessarily the Christ, and his humanity is thereby downplayed, then the so-called New Covenant actually looks remarkably and depressingly similar to the Old Covenant, except that God has now revealed himself as Three Persons in one God, rather than remaining as the more monolithic Jahweh of the Old Covenant. Apart from this, the actual basis of the covenant has changed little, if at all. The situation is what it always was, and the author of Ecclesiastes got it right that, 'there is nothing new under the sun' (1:9).

For in such a covenant it is still a relationship between the entirely fixed and separate ontological categories of human and divine: us as the new people of the covenant, and God (including the implausibly human and actually in practical terms entirely divine Jesus Christ) as the bestower of the blessings of salvation and eternal life. The promise of the blessing may be new, but the form of the covenant itself is not: it is no more a covenant of genuine partnership between divinity and humanity than the Old Covenant ever was – just as, in fact, from within the parameters

of traditional christological methods, neither could be the incarnation itself.

By contrast, a christology of becoming genuinely does allow
for the ushering in of an entirely new covenant through the life,
death and resurrection of Jesus of Nazareth, thereafter also
known as the Christ. For in a Jesus Christ conceived of in such a
way, we see human and divine eternally and genuinely united,
and the New Covenant is enfleshed and personified in him as a
perfect partnership. Human obedience and divine blessing are
now for all time one in him. The Old Testament covenants of
trust, faithfulness and love have now become a new covenant of
indwelling.

In a moment we must turn to the consequences of this for
ourselves as the people of the covenant, but first it is worth noting that this perfect mutual indwelling of human and divine in
Jesus Christ also makes a great deal more sense of one of the
New Testament's favourite images, that of the mediator. In particular this image is favoured by the author of the Epistle to the
Hebrews, and it is, of course, entirely relevant to the idea of
covenant since it is precisely this New Covenant of which Jesus
is said to be the mediator.

Curiously, there are I think only two occasions on which
Hebrews uses the actual word 'mediator'. These occur at 8:6
('But Jesus has now obtained a more excellent ministry, and to
that degree he is the mediator of a better covenant, which has
been enacted through better promises'), and at 12:22-24: ('But
you have come ... to Jesus, the mediator of a new covenant').
Standing powerfully behind these explicit uses of the word,
though, there is the extended metaphor of the High Priesthood
of Jesus Christ, 'a priest for ever after the order of Melchizedek',
and the figure of the priest was, of course, the mediator *par excel-
lence* between humankind and God.

For the priests of the Old Covenant, although they stood as
mediators, the relationship was the inevitably unequal one of
human and divine. Traditional christology does not even
achieve this much: indeed, it may be argued that it depicts not a
New Covenant, but a retrograde step in the covenant relationship, since the thoroughly swamped humanity of Jesus can
hardly be said to be a willing party to anything at all.

In a christology of becoming, Jesus as the Christ is seen as the perfect mediator – human becomes divine and the two are forever conjoined, and the exalted (but entirely real) humanity of Jesus which has ever said 'Yes' to God is able for all time to intercede for the failings of those who truly are his brothers and sisters. Here now, within the Godhead, with Jesus as its mediator, is a New Covenant of perfect partnership. It is, if you like, to return to the Old Adam/New Adam image discussed earlier, a return to that perfect partnership which was originally envisaged by God, and which, once undone by human sin, is now restored by human faithfulness.

This realisation that Jesus inaugurates and mediates a New Covenant of partnership leads us to the final – but vital – issue in connection with covenant: what does this radically new covenant in Jesus Christ imply for us as the people of that covenant?

Quite simply, the implications are immense, and for us (and we may even dare to say for God too, since we are no longer dealing with an impassible and therefore unchanging God) life-changing. Once again, as with previous issues, it is worth comparing the outlook engendered by a christology of becoming with that produced by any more traditional christological method.

In traditional christologies, we have argued time and again, it is quite impossible to do full justice to the humanity of Jesus – as we have seen, the human party to the mediation of the New Covenant is overwhelmed by the divine and there is no genuine partnership, no fully reciprocal relationship. If this is the case with the mediator of the covenant himself, then how can we ever hope to enter fully into covenant partnership with God? Yes, we may receive his blessings, and yes, one may still strive to remain faithful to him, but this is still only the grossly unequal Old Covenant writ large.

As in so many areas, though, all is different if we will once allow for the possibility of a christology of becoming. And the principal reason for this difference is that such a christology takes entirely seriously the human nature of Jesus Christ – even to the point of asserting, as we have done, that the human nature of Jesus could have refused to become, or simply failed to become, the Christ.

At this point two central facts coinhere and coalesce into one great truth, which, like the concept of Jesus as mediator, is richly reflected in New Testament image and metaphor. The first fact is that Jesus was utterly human – one of us – and not a human being who, unlike any other human being, had no choice but to be what he was. Jesus was like us to the extent that his entire life was, like ours, contingent: it could have been entirely different and nothing had to be as it was. The second fact, usually expressed in the form that Jesus shares our human nature, which, as we have seen is only true for a christology of becoming, is actually better expressed for the purposes of explaining its consequences, in the form that we share Jesus' human nature.

These facts – that Jesus' life shares in the contingency of our lives, and that Jesus' human nature truly is our human nature, open up an entirely new perspective on the idea of covenant, and one which makes the New Covenant genuinely new. For the first time, through the perfected (but still real) humanity of Jesus Christ, the covenant is a genuine partnership. And, as we share in the same human nature as Jesus, we share more fully in this covenant than in any previous one; and as a consequence, one of the great New Testament images can begin to resonate fully within us for the very first time.

This image is one particularly beloved of St Paul, and it is that of us as sons (or in more inclusive language, children) and heirs of God by virtue of our being the brothers and sisters of Jesus Christ. It has always been, potentially at least, a powerful and evocative image, but christology's consistent failure to do full justice to the humanity of Jesus has never allowed it to take full root in our hearts and souls. But with a christology of becoming this can at last happen. Jesus is 'like us' and we are therefore his brothers and sisters and can own the name of children and heirs of God.

This recovery of the concept of covenant, and with it the rejuvenation of so much rich New Testament imagery, is one of the great consequential benefits of espousing a christology of becoming. Covenant has always been – and still is – a key idea within Judaism, but it is hardly surprising that it is one which, within Christianity, has long ceased to resonate with all but a small coterie of theologians: and should the truth of this be doubted, just try asking the average 'person in the pew' what significance the concept of covenant has for them! Perhaps at last, with the assistance of a new method of doing christology, this ancient and evocative depiction of our relationship with God can be once again restored to life and enabled to resume its rightful place among the conceptual furnishings of our faith.

Such a rediscovery of the richness of covenant imagery might do much to invigorate faith in an era of accidie and scepticism, but as well as having implications for our spiritual lives and sense of identity as a covenant people, a christology of becoming also impinges upon our ethical outlook and our ecclesiology, particularly in terms of what we might call the church's 'foreign policy' as it relates to other faiths. These issues therefore form the substance of the following two chapters.

CHAPTER THIRTEEN

'No Sex Please – We're Christians'

In the first part of this study we explored with some thorough-
ness the doctrines of original sin and original guilt and the related
issues of the virginal conception of Jesus and the supposed need
to shield him from any taint imparted by even the faintest whiff of
human sexuality. In this discussion we were concerned primarily
with the doctrinal implications, but here we need to re-visit some
of the same territory in order to establish what impact a christology of becoming might have upon our sense of ourselves and
our identity as engendered, and therefore, sexual beings.

There is little point in repeating here the substance of our
grievance with St Augustine, other than to reiterate the fact that
his legacy (and that of so many others of the first few centuries,
to say nothing of later epochs) has been almost entirely negative
with regard to the whole realm of human sexuality.

The forms of this negativity have been many and various,
but two central themes (re-worked through the ages in any
number of ways) stand out. Between them they appear, unfortunately but accurately, to portray Christianity as generally misanthropic and specifically misogynistic – which may, incidentally,
go a long way towards explaining the otherwise inexplicable
continuing resistance towards the ordination of women.

The misanthropic outlook of Christianity has been exemplified in its attempt simply to write off a major aspect of our God-
given nature – that is, our sexuality – as intrinsically evil. It can
be argued that this even began in the Bible, with St Paul's advice
to virgins to remain thus, with the somewhat grudging proviso
that if, in spite of his advice, they do decide to marry, they 'do
not sin', this being part of his generally negative advice concerning marriage in 1 Corinthians 7:25-35.

It was, however, the great patristic authors who wove this
particular strand so spectacularly into the fabric of Christianity.

Essentially the denigration of human sexuality occurred on two fronts simultaneously: one simply as a result of negativity, the other as a negative spin-off from an otherwise largely positive development.

The purely negative movement was that associated with the developing doctrine of the Fall, which reached its climax, as we have argued in Part One of this study, in the thinking of St Augustine. To be fair to St Augustine, however, he was only giving final shape and form to a corpus of ideas which had been floating around for a long time. In his thinking, though, the partial and inchoate thoughts of others became all too clearly defined.

We have discovered the reasons for St Augustine's views on sexuality earlier, but whatever the psychological motivation for them may have been, there is no doubt that for St Augustine and for many of the other early Christian writers, human sexuality was intrinsically evil. This evil is, for them, portrayed graphically in the story of Adam and Eve.

Adam and Eve are created innocent: that is, we must presume that they are sexual beings from the first, but they do not even know that they are naked. Presumably, therefore, whatever there is of sexual desire is likewise innocent. Certainly there is no sense of shame or guilt inhering in the relationship between Adam and Eve before the Fall. Afterwards, though, all is utterly different.

The key moment is Adam's 'confession' when he hears the sound of the Lord God walking in the garden in the cool of the evening, and his response is: 'I was afraid because I was naked and I hid myself' (Genesis 3:10). From this point on human sexuality, from the point of view of any positive appreciation, is doomed. The best one can hope for is that the beast can be, if not exactly tamed, at least regulated. Thus was developed the all-encompassing and all too often repressive Christian code of sexual ethics.

All of this ingrained negativity towards sexuality was then given a further twist through the impact of a movement which was, of itself, largely positive – monasticism. The monastic movement began, essentially, with the solitary asceticism of the Desert Fathers, but the monastic ideal quickly took root and flourished wherever Christianity prospered, and what began as a Middle Eastern and North African practice came, within a few hundred years, to be a distinctive feature of Christian life all across Europe, and monasticism can genuinely be said to have shaped the destiny of Christianity for the best part of a thousand years.

The connection between the rise of monasticism and the denigration of human sexuality is all too obvious. Clearly, one of the traditional monastic vows is that of celibacy. This, in itself, need not be a problem; but damaging consequences came about as soon as the monastic life was perceived as being in any way 'superior' to or 'better' than a secular life. Celibacy rapidly became synonymous with virtue, and sexual activity therefore became, if not exactly a vice, at least a second best option and an admission of imperfection. Sex, to paraphrase the words of *1066 And All That* was definitely not 'A Good Thing'.

However, Christianity is responsible not merely for a somewhat gloomy picture of the human sexual situation, but also for a thoroughly negative assessment – which still has repercussions to this day – of the status and inherent nature of women.

The trouble all began with Eve – or at least that is what the weight of patristic tradition would have us believe. Poor Eve! In front of an exclusively male judge and jury she is unanimously found guilty on two counts. First, she and not Adam was the 'original sinner'. The serpent may have been clever and she may have been deceived, but in spite of this she nonetheless willingly and culpably transgressed the explicit commandment of God about not eating the fruit of a particular tree.

Secondly, and perhaps even more importantly, it was she who caused Adam to fall. Adam had resisted eating the forbidden fruit – indeed the story gives no indication that he had even felt any temptation to eat it – until he is presented with it by Eve. Her transgression was directly responsible for his, and she is therefore doubly culpable.

This second count of guilt has had a lasting and thoroughly pernicious spin-off effect on Christianity's perception of female sexuality in particular: this episode being the blueprint for woman as temptress. Certainly during the patristic period – and indeed for long after as well – women were seen as full of an unbridled sexual desire which they were entirely unable properly to control, with the result that every woman represented a permanent temptation to poor, weak, fallen men. Female sexuality (and therefore by extension, sexuality in general) was something to be feared and, for the most part, shunned.

This negative vision of human sexuality exists in a reciprocally strengthening relationship with all traditional forms of christology. There is a direct correlation between the Fall (with its realisation of nakedness and implied awareness of sexuality) and Christianity's insistence on the virginal conception of Jesus Christ. Each reinforces and validates the other, depending upon which is taken as being the first term of the equation.

Thus if the Fall (complete with its Augustinian connotations of original guilt) is the first term, then it is obvious that the Christ cannot possibly be held to be tainted in this way. Ergo, he must have been virginally conceived, and, indeed, for Roman Catholics at least, his mother was also immaculately conceived in order to provide a double shield.

Conversely, if the virginal conception of Jesus is given first place, then it raises the question of what the terrible thing is from which Jesus needed to be protected, and the answer, plainly, is the sin and guilt transmitted by means of human sexuality. Either way, the incarnation and human sexuality are incompatible, and the perfection of the one only goes to show up the imperfection (at best) or innate sinfulness (at worst) of the other.

For a christology of becoming, however, there is no such radical disjunction and therefore no such opposition between incarnation and sexuality. Once the doctrine of original sin has been shorn of its Augustinian terrors there is no longer any need to fear sexuality *per se*, and there is no good reason why – as is also far more likely – Jesus should not have been born to Mary and Joseph in the normal way.

Such a reunification of the realms of incarnation and sexuality also has wider ramifications for the whole question of the relationship between matter and spirit in Christianity, and this also ties back in to our earlier discussion of monasticism with its renunciation of the things of the flesh.

More or less consistently throughout Christian history, matter has been conceived of as being opposed to spirit and inferior to it, and the obvious 'fleshliness' of sexuality has been viewed as a key index of this opposition. Once we can begin to appreciate our sexuality without the burdens of original sin and original guilt, however, the whole spirit/matter opposition is called into question. One need not be seen as being somehow 'better' than the other: they are simply different. Moreover, as C. S. Lewis eloquently puts it: 'God likes matter – he invented it.'[1]

An acceptance of a christology of becoming, with its concomitant revision of our outlook on sexuality, sin and guilt, spirit and matter, has huge consequences for us. To begin with, there is the affirmation that we are no longer condemned to see ourselves as products of an inferior creation; a creation tainted in particular by its necessary but regrettable participation in enfleshment and specifically sexuality. In this connection it is not too much to claim that mainstream Christianity – for all its avowed abhorrence towards anything which smacks of heterodoxy – has always been subtly and deleteriously influenced by the theological flavour, even if not the specific doctrines, of the early Gnostic sects.

At their most extreme, these sects, in their determination to set up the most powerful opposition possible between spirit and matter, argued that the material world was the creation of what they called the 'demiurge' – a secondary, inferior and possibly even evil divine being whose efforts in creation had actually hindered the perfect intentions of the necessarily perfect supreme being. All that was left of his goodness in humanity was a spiritual divine 'spark', and the whole purpose of the religious life was, by means of esoteric gnosis, to foster this spark until finally matter was subdued and divine spirit could reign supreme.

Clearly these doctrines are heretical, and Christianity has stuck firmly to its formula of God as Trinity, and the demiurge has been thoroughly excised from the picture and consigned to the 'sin-bin' of history. And yet ... And yet the flavour of dissatisfaction with our enfleshed and material state remains, and it is somehow to be escaped from and transcended until we arrive at our real home in the world of spirit.

Within an ontological framework governed by a christology of becoming, however, none of this pertains any longer. Matter is not inferior to spirit, and we, as human beings of infinite

potential (just as Jesus was) are sharers in God's mode of incarnation. Jesus, as we saw in the previous chapter, becomes more
literally our brother, and if God is capable of becoming incarnate in a human being conceived in the normal way, then what
became reality in Jesus lives also as a potential within the rest of
us. Our human flesh is enabled, if only we will, as Jesus did, say
'Yes' to God and go on saying 'Yes', to become tinged with the
divine.

This insight and aspiration is not a new one, but it is one
which has hitherto surfaced to any significant extent only within
the esoteric and rarefied world of medieval mysticism – within
which, of course, the usual Christian matter/spirit distinction
still largely applied also. Nonetheless, many of the great mystics, perhaps especially Hildegard of Bingen and Meister
Eckhart did give genuine voice to the possibility of human
union with the divine. For them such a vision was realised when
spirit conquered matter, and the enfleshed soul was sufficiently
freed from its chains to attain communion with a higher realm.
A similar insight has continued to surface from time to time
(largely within the monastic traditions) down to the present day
in figures such as Thomas Merton, but always the matter/spirit
disjunction has been, whether overtly or implicitly, firmly main-
tained.

A fully human enfleshed Christ of becoming changes all of
this. Traditional christology has always held up to us a Christ
who is so spiritual – because necessarily divine – that there is no
question of matter or embodiedness getting in the way, and it
leaves us, therefore, with the feeling that our own very obvious
embodiedness puts us at a spiritual disadvantage and must be
overcome. With a fully humanly embodied Christ of becoming,
spirit no longer has to overcome matter and we are no longer
burdened with the suspicion (or certainty, depending upon
your theological and ecclesiastical standpoint) that matter must
be so defeated precisely because it is intrinsically inferior or
even evil.

Far more positively, the equation between matter and spirit
may now be expressed in entirely different terms. For now we
may say that matter has the inherent and God-given potential to
work with the spirit, and we are no longer constrained to say

that matter is *de facto* against spirit. Rather than the scenario
being that spirit has to overcome matter, we may now say that
spirit and matter need simply (but Oh! so elusively) to be one in
their never-ending 'Yes' to God. When this happens, as in Jesus
Christ, then at last humanity and divinity truly meet in incarnation, both two thousand years ago, and derivatively and as the
ultimate aspiration of our humanity, today in us as his followers.

A christology of becoming thus certainly improves the state
of things in the church's 'home affairs' department, but it equally
impinges, as we noted at the close of the previous chapter, upon
its 'foreign affairs' department – in other words the potential of
the various churches to engage in mission to those outside them,
and the relationships between these churches and the wider
realm of the other world faiths. It is therefore upon this wider
prospect that we must now, at least briefly, reflect.

Notes
1. C. S. Lewis, *Mere Christianity*, London, Collins, Fontana Books,
Twentieth Impression, 1972, p 62, (First pub 1952).

CHAPTER FOURTEEN

Les Liaisons Dangereuses

All faiths are inherently conservative and, almost by definition, convinced of their own rightness: after all, you do not continue to believe in something if you are convinced that it is misguided or inaccurate. In this respect Christianity is no different from any other faith: indeed, it may be argued that as a direct result of its core beliefs, including christology, it is actually more doctrinally entrenched than almost any other of the world faiths.

This doctrinal rigidity operates in two spheres. First, it is a factor in the relationships between the various Christian denominations. For example, do we consider that the threefold order of ministry is of the *esse* of the true church, or that the Blessed Virgin Mary was immaculately conceived and assumed into heaven, or that the Holy Spirit proceeds from the Father alone or from both the Father and the Son? Each Christian denomination has its own distinctive confessional beliefs and each is naturally convinced of its own rightness over against the position of others.

Secondly, and even more significantly, what is true on the confessional scale of relationships between denominations is writ large when it comes to Christianity's relationships with the other world faiths. On the surface, relationships, at least in recent years, are cordial. Gone – thankfully – are the days of the Crusades or the systematic persecution of the Jews by Christians. Now the Pope meets with the leaders of other faiths and prays with them in Assisi; Muslims, Jews and Christians hold inter-faith conferences and seminars; and in practical terms aid agencies co-operate in relief and development work wherever there is need regardless of belief. Underneath all of this, though – and it may, from their perspective, be equally true of the other faiths – there is, on the part of Christianity, an ultimate conviction of innate superiority. The (largely unspoken) attitude is that whilst other faiths may have wonderful practices, such as particular techniques for meditation, and some useful insights, nonetheless they ultimately fall short of Christianity's revelation of God in Jesus Christ. If they have any salvific value it is of a 'back door' variety – that is, if they are lucky, God will probably not reject the well-meaning if misguided intentions and beliefs of these other faiths.

Furthermore, and it is part of the reason why a re-estimate such as we have been advocating in the present volume is necessary, much of Christianity's doctrinal rigidity hinges upon its approach to christology. For Christianity tenaciously – and unhelpfully – clings to two particular tenets with regard to the person and work of Jesus Christ which profoundly hamper both its mission and its capacity fully to respect the validity and salvific status of any other faith.

The first of these, which is of course the subject of the substance of this study, relates to the essential nature of Jesus Christ. For two thousand years Christianity has assumed – largely thanks to the ontological constraints of classical metaphysics – that Jesus had to be the Christ, that he was, philosophically speaking, necessarily who he was. Clearly, if this is so, and if the child in the manger just *is* the Christ, then he is, because God has willed it so, the only one who can reveal to us anything of God in human form; whereas, for a Christ of becoming the case is, as we shall see in due course, somewhat different.

The second tenet, which we have discussed in terms of its theological veracity in Chapter 10, is the claim that Christ died 'for the forgiveness of sins'. Again, if this is correct it makes Christianity the only possible true faith since no other figure is recorded as having claimed to do this. Even more to the point, in terms of the exclusivity of Christianity, if this is true then there is no possibility of salvation by any other means. All other faiths are instantly ruled out, and statements such as 'I am the way, the truth and the life' and 'No-one comes to the Father except by me' (John 14:6) become literally, and by definition for other faiths, denigratingly, true.

Although both of these tenets impact on a variety of areas of the church's work and witness, it would be fair to say that the first relates especially to mission, and the second to the relationship of Christianity to the other major world faiths. And, in each case, a re-evaluation of christology such as we have advocated here makes an immense and entirely creative difference to Christianity's position.

First, then, mission – and it must be clearly understood what is meant by this term. Indeed, it is possibly a term which the church would do well to get away from, for it is freighted with outdated and largely negative connotations. The word 'mission' conjures up a vision of pith helmets and colonial values and the imparting of a culture (and supposed civilisation) as much as the preaching of a faith.

Today, however, the reality behind the word 'mission' is altogether different. We live in a post-Christian world where the majority of the population is almost entirely unchurched, and the level of ignorance about Christianity and the Bible (even in terms merely of its cultural rather than specifically religious significance) is higher than ever before. For example, I know of a teacher who discovered, while teaching on Milton's *Paradise Lost* that ninety-five percent of her class had never even heard of Adam and Eve.

This is the situation, in the west at least, in which the church finds itself working; and coupled with this basic lack of knowledge of Christianity is a widespread perception that the church is a 'closed shop' – that in order to join one has to sign up to a complete package and assent to every last tiny part of it. It is a little like buying an airline ticket on the internet: before the deal is concluded you must tick the 'I assent to the terms and conditions' box.

In such a situation, a new approach to christology could prove transformative. The reason why this is so is quite simply that it could re-connect christology with the vast bulk of the – currently alienated or negative – population. For the reality is that whilst only a small percentage of the population are actively members of a church, surveys (and statistics of religious book publishing) indicate that many more people would describe themselves as 'religious' and as being on some kind of spiritual journey or search. These are the people to whom the church should have – and, with the right christology, could have – a mission.

A christology of becoming could richly facilitate such a mission. The trouble with traditional christologies in which Jesus is necessarily the Christ is the rigidity of their doctrinal framework – the package necessarily includes such things as the virginal conception of Jesus; and there are undoubtedly many people who are at least interested in the person of Jesus but who could not, as Lewis Carroll's character Alice puts it, believe 'as many as six impossible things before breakfast'. For such people a christology of becoming has the potential to transform everything. Such a christology is intrinsically more flexible than traditional models, and as a result many doctrinal boundaries similarly become more flexible and there is room for differences of opinion and for people to explore the magnetic personality of Jesus without having first to assent to an exclusive and exhaustive package of beliefs.

The atmosphere is almost automatically more conducive towards some form of belief for the potentially vast constituency of those who are spiritually searching, but are currently (and hardly surprisingly) unchurched. For all too many of these people, I suspect, the major problem is the church's perceived identity as being what I have described as a 'Dispensing Church' – that is, a church which believes that it has all the doctrinal and ethical answers and simply tells its adherents precisely what to believe and how to behave.

For the many people who are uncomfortable with such a model of church, a christology of becoming might prove to be a vital means of reconnecting with the person – and therefore also with the work – of Jesus Christ. And the principal reason why this may be so is that a christology of becoming restores the full and dynamic humanity of Jesus which has for so long been at best downplayed and at worst completely stifled by christology's insistence on the prior and overwhelming divinity of the Christ. In the case of a Jesus who is necessarily the Christ, the rapid accretion of rigid beliefs becomes necessary also, and these beliefs largely serve to obscure his humanity precisely because they are designed to emphasise his divinity.

If, however, we can make room for a Jesus who becomes the Christ through the freely chosen co-operation of his humanity with God, then a refreshing and life-enhancing relaxation of dogmatic boundaries is facilitated. We are, for example, as we have seen, no longer required to believe in the virginal conception of Jesus, or to take the temptation narratives at their face value. Certainly the core belief remains that Jesus is the Christ, but a much wider range of interpretation of his person and his work becomes possible, and the doctrinally remote figure of the Christ becomes newly accessible in the compelling person of Jesus-bar-Joseph.

A christology of becoming thus has the potential to revitalise mission, but it has even more far-reaching implications for the future of Christianity's relationship with the other world faiths, implications which amount to a complete paradigm shift in terms of Christianity's own perception of this relationship.

Such a shift is brought about by two things in particular, one of which relates primarily to the person and the other to the work of Jesus Christ. First, the person. According to any traditional account of christology, the person of Jesus Christ is not merely unique but actively exclusive. God has chosen to become incarnate in this one individual, complete with a miraculous conception, and there is no point of comparison with any of the other significant figures in the world faiths – they are, by definition, inferior because not divine.

Our understanding of the person of Jesus Christ is, though, transformed by means of a christology of becoming, as is his relationship to such religious leaders and teachers as the Prophet Mohammed and the Buddha. For if Jesus became the Christ through the ongoing 'Yes' of his humanity toward God then, although he remains unique as the Christ (this being, as we argued in Chapter Seven a specific and 'once off' vocation, just as every human being's vocation to be uniquely themselves is), nonetheless the achievement of his humanity in this becoming validates rather than downplays the holiness and sanctity of the great leaders of other faiths. It remains true that Jesus' status as the Christ continues to be normative for Christianity, but there is no reason why his response of 'Yes' to God should not manifest itself likewise in others. Indeed, there is every reason to suppose that, whether or not the name of Jesus is invoked or recognised, such a 'Yes' to God is the vocation of every human being. This being the case, there is room in a christology of becoming for other great 'Yes' sayers, and why should not the Prophet Mohammed and the Buddha stand as inspirational icons of the potential greatness of the human spirit precisely as Jesus himself does?

Likewise, just as Christianity's relationship with and view of other faiths is radically altered by a fresh understanding of the person of Jesus Christ, so too it is creatively transformed by a re-evaluation of his work. In a previous chapter we have argued for precisely such a re-evaluation, contending that the principal work accomplished by him was not a death 'for the forgiveness of sins' but a reconciliation, through his perpetual 'Yes' to God, between the human and the divine.

The traditional 'for the forgiveness of sins' motif has two profound shortcomings, one purely internal to Christianity which we will glance at only briefly, and one which impinges with great and negative significance on Christianity's ability to relate to other faiths. At the level of Christianity's own internal rationale, then, the idea that Jesus' defining work was that he 'died for the forgiveness of sins' (quite apart from the fact that it calls into question the nature of a God who requires such a death in order to forgive) immediately makes this death virtually the entire purpose of Jesus' whole life: he lived simply in order to die. Conversely, the situation is remedied if reconciliation is viewed as being his primary work, for this involves literally the whole of his life as well as his death, for it was a reconciliation which was wrought on a daily basis as every moment of 'Yes' to God brought the humanity of the man Jesus ever closer to the divine.

More importantly for our purposes here, though, the doctrine that Jesus died for 'the forgiveness of sins' is prejudicial to Christianity's estimation of other faiths. For if this doctrine is correct then the salvific value of all other faiths is impugned and all are, as it were, in debt to Christianity for achieving a salvation which they are themselves quite incapable of attaining. This is necessarily so simply because if Jesus did indeed live principally in order to die for the forgiveness of sins then the world is ontologically changed by that death, and all that we can do is to take or leave that forgiveness; and it is to be assumed that, because they have not been willing to invoke the name of Jesus

Christ, other faiths have chosen to leave it rather than take it – although they may, of course, yet be saved as a result of Jesus' death through the universality of God's mercy which makes allowances for human shortcomings of belief, as of conduct.

This picture is unflattering to say the least, and to the adherents of the other world faiths it regularly comes across as condescending and derogatory. Everything changes, however – and very much for the better – if we posit Jesus' chief work as being that of reconciliation, and if we allow that this was a work which spanned the whole of his life in its 'Yes' to God rather than being focused (as with the forgiveness of sins) on an ontologically seismic death. Dying for the forgiveness of sins is a once-off event (forgiveness was not there before but is now), and one in which we can only participate as grateful recipients of that forgiveness. By contrast, if Jesus lived and died in order to forge a reconciliation between the human and the divine (to form, that is, by obedience the 'New Adam' of St Paul's typology) and if he stands as an icon of that perfect reconciliation, then others are thereby empowered to share in that same work by being bearers of reconciliation themselves – and that reconciliation remains equally valid whether the name of Jesus Christ is explicitly invoked or not. By their prayers, practices and ethics all of the world faiths are engaged upon this great work, and all, therefore, share the salvific reality which Christianity has too often abrogated to itself alone.

Both from the point of view of mission to the unchurched and from the perspective of the genuineness of Christianity's conversations with other faiths, then, a christology of becoming with its contingent rather than necessary Christ has much to commend itself. The difference between Christ's necessity or contingency in the context of both mission and inter-faith dialogue is easily summarised.

Thus, a Jesus who is necessarily the Christ – as christology has always previously insisted upon – is equally necessarily and by definition the only possible one who must be followed in order to gain salvation, especially if his death is interpreted as being the key point of his life and as being for the forgiveness of sins.

Conversely, what a contrast is revealed if we take away the

necessity for Jesus to be the Christ and allow for the sheer and glorious contingency of becoming. This Christ is one who reveals the full potential of our humanity and holds out a vision of how we might be, and does so in a non-exclusive way, and, therefore, beside others who stand, for the adherents of other faiths, equally as icons of human and divine co-operation and reconciliation.

In essence what is being suggested here – and what is made possible by a christology of becoming – is a re-estimation and re-evaluation of the relative importance of the person and work of Jesus Christ. Traditionally christology has insisted that we must first believe correctly in the identity of the person of Jesus Christ before we can be partakers in, or beneficiaries of his work. A christology of becoming, by contrast, prioritises his work and proclaims that it is precisely this work – of reconciliation – which forged Jesus' contingent identity as the Christ.

And the consequences of this for mission and inter-faith dialogue are little short of momentous. Christianity itself will still maintain its attachment to and devotion for his person, but its proclamation in mission and the starting point for its dialogue with other faiths will henceforth be that it is his *way* – that of reconciliation with God, which is also the way of other religious figures – which must be followed rather than, necessarily and as a prior condition, his *person*. Christianity will proclaim, both in mission and in dialogue, that Jesus' path of a daily, hourly, minutely 'Yes' to God is 'the way, the truth and the life', but it will also acknowledge that as it was this manner of life which made real the person of the Christ, so too it is this same manner of life rather than the consequent and contingent person which is, ultimately, crucial. By such means Christianity is brought into a new and richly creative relationship with those of all faiths and none.

CONCLUSION

Apologia Pro Libra Sua

As I began to write this book I was aware, as I mentioned in the Introduction, of the temerity of venturing into the minefield of christology. I am even more aware of it now, having explored at least some of the territory and as this work draws to a close. More precisely, I am aware that I am arguing in the face of a two thousand year old tradition as to how christology should be done and what its presuppositions may be taken as being. We may not any longer have ecumenical councils pronouncing upon the finer points of Trinitarian or christological doctrine, but there remains a well-ensconced theological establishment which is firmly wedded to tried and tested theological methods and concepts.

The problem is, however – and I suspect is for many people and not just for me – that these methods and concepts are rooted in a world which has long since vanished and ceased to have any real meaning. The world in question is, of course, that of Greek and Latin metaphysics and associated ontological specu-lation, and for most of us today this world is archaic and foreign in the extreme.

Hence the need for the present work. There is a pressing re-quirement for Christianity, and in particular christology, to 'think outside the box', for christology certainly, if not the en-tirety of Christianity, has been confined within this particular metaphysical box for too long and has become tired and stale as a result.

And the most tragic aspect of all is that as Christian doctrine has mouldered and mildewed, so faith itself has come to seem outmoded and fit only for those who, for whatever reasons of retreat from reality, are content to live in this dust-covered archive from history. The decline of faith is due primarily not to the rise of a supposedly anti-religious scientific worldview or to the relativism of the so-called post-modern world, but to Christianity's own self-inflicted fossilisation.

There seems little doubt that at the present time, in the west at least, Christianity is at a crossroads. One option is that it sticks grimly to its ultra-traditional guns and continues to atrophy by degrees until – if there is anyone left who actually bothers to notice – it disappears from view. The other option is to re-cast the good news (gospel) of God in Jesus Christ in contemporary categories of thought in such a way that the events of two thousand years ago come to life once more in the hearts, minds and imaginations of a new generation. This way there may lie ahead a new resurrection of faith in an age in which, for many, that faith in its traditional guise at least, seems to have died.

Traditionalists will argue that to do this is unthinkable, and the aroma of burning heretics will wistfully be imagined: but why should the doctrines of our ancient faith – and, as being so central to it, christology in particular – not be thus re-cast and re-envisioned? A living faith must be free to articulate new categories of thought and new models. Indeed, not to do so would, ironically, actually be to play false to the deepest insights of those Greek and Latin metaphysical theologians from whose thrall we are now trying to free ourselves. For what they were doing was to attempt to express the data of scripture and personal experience of God in Jesus Christ in the current conceptual framework of their day.

And, in our own generation, why should we not be free to do the same? We cannot remain shackled forever to just one theological language and one set of theological concepts, even one which contains such hoary and venerable ideas as *ousia, hypostasis, perona, prosopon* and so on. Those who wish to remain with these concepts would no doubt argue that they are not only ancient but somehow also 'right'. As the song from George Gershwin's *Porgy and Bess* says, however, this 'ain't necessarily so', and we need to set before ourselves very clearly the nature and scope of the task of theology.

For it is all too easy to assume that the formulations such as those of the councils of Chalcedon, Nicea and so on just 'are' – once pronounced they are definitive and remain the only acceptable way of expressing our understanding of Christian doctrine. What we need always to remember, though, is that however useful these formulations and concepts may once have been, they are not now and never have been 'exact' or factual descriptions of the nature of Jesus or of the Trinity or of anything else. By definition when we are dealing with anything pertaining to the nature of God, we are dealing with things which are ultimately beyond our finite understanding. We cannot adequately either understand or express the divine in human concepts. Certainly some may appear to us to be more useful than others, but none will ever exactly match that ineffable reality which it seeks to explore.

Since, then, one can never say that theology is telling the exact truth about God – such exact truth being unavailable to us – then we must conclude that even the best and most profound theology is composed of models: that is, images and concepts which allow us to glimpse at least something of what the Trinity or the divine/human nature of Jesus Christ might be said to be like. We cannot insist on the absolute 'rightness' of any formulation of doctrine, for no such formulation is possible for us.

The reality is that theology works with models – and the truth is that models can be changed. Precisely because they are not exact, neither are they immutable. They may prove useful for long periods of time, but if they become tired or antiquated then newer and more vibrant ones may legitimately replace them – or at least be set up alongside them.

This is precisely what is needed now in the realm of christology, and is what has been at least attempted here. For its own sake, Christianity cannot afford to remain rigidly locked into an outmoded thought world and maintain that there is no other language in which its theology may legitimately be done. There must be other languages than ancient metaphysics and fixed ontological categories in which to express the wonders and mysteries of our faith, and in the present case especially the incarnation.

Exploring new concepts and categories of thought is intrinsic to the well-being of a living faith, and after all there is already diversity in the worldwide church about such a central issue as the procession of the Holy Spirit – and if there is diversity with regard to this model then why should there not be a similar diversity with regard to other models? In the case of the Holy Spirit, the eastern church maintains the doctrine of a single procession (from the Father alone), while the west champions a double procession, from the Father and from the Son. Both, presumably, cannot be right, and one part of the church must therefore be presumed to be in a state of sincere error. But is this so awful a place to be, and will God ultimately condemn one part of the church for an 'incorrect' (and therefore, strictly speaking, heretical) belief. No: for each model is just that; a model which is designed to illuminate what each part of the church perceives as being a valuable insight into the nature of the relationships within the Holy Trinity.

Similarly, this volume attempts to articulate a new method of doing christology in order to create a model which might creatively illuminate both the relationship of Jesus of Nazareth with the second person of the Trinity, (the Son, the Word, the Christ) and our own relationship with God through him. The model developed and delineated here may or may not prove to be a useful one. It may or may not produce resonances and further new ideas and articulations of these ideas in others. The value of the model of a christology of becoming is for others to decide. But the creation of such new models is, however, I believe, an essential task which lies at the heart of the theological endeavour, and in the undertaking of which lies the best hope of proffering a rich and vibrant vision of our faith to each and every new generation of potential believers. Such at least was the spirit and belief in which this book was both begun and ended, and in which the model which it describes is offered to the community of believers and, very importantly also, enquirers, for their prayerful consideration.

Index of Names